SH**GED.
MARRIED.
ANNOYED.

SH**GED.
MARRIED.
ANNOYED.

CHRIS & ROSIE RAMSEY

MICHAEL JOSEPH
an imprint of
PENGUIN BOOKS

MICHAEL JOSEPH

UK | USA | Canada | Ireland | Australia
India | New Zealand | South Africa

Michael Joseph is part of the Penguin Random House group of companies
whose addresses can be found at global.penguinrandomhouse.com

First published by Michael Joseph 2020
001

Set in 12.5/16 pt Granjon LT Std,
13.5/16 pt Garamond MT Std,
10/16 pt Frutiger Neue LT Book,
11.5/16 pt Roble Light
Typeset by Jouve (UK), Milton Keynes
Printed and bound in Great Britain by Clays Ltd, Elcograf S.p.A.

A CIP catalogue record for this book is available from the British Library

ISBN: 978-0-241-44712-3

www.greenpenguin.co.uk

MIX
Paper from
responsible sources
FSC® C018179

Penguin Random House is committed to a
sustainable future for our business, our readers
and our planet. This book is made from Forest
Stewardship Council® certified paper.

For our Robin. Mammy and Daddy love you with all our hearts. Please never read this book.

Introduction

Hello,

You're ~~listening to~~ READING Sh**ged. Married. Annoyed. ~~With~~ BY Chris and Rosie Ramsey.

And we're so happy that you're here!

This book is all about the ups and downs, the ins and outs, the highs and lows of life, relationships, families and everything in-between. This is not a self-help book. It contains no advice that you should follow yourself. We, like everyone else out there, have absolutely no idea what we're doing when it comes to life . . . we don't have the answers. But what we do have is the ability to talk about life and take the piss out of it. And that is what this is.

It's a piss-take.

The fact that Rosie Ramsey (formerly Rosie Winter) and Chris Ramsey (always Chris Ramsey) are even writing a book is a piss-take in itself. Our respective English teachers at school will be flabbergasted that this is happening. And we are too.

We started our podcast of the same name to have a laugh, vent at each other and at the world. We wanted to talk about the things we found interesting. The things we found funny. The things we found disgusting. We had no agenda or plan, but it's spiralled into something we couldn't have imagined.

Millions of downloads and entertained ears later, we have a book. And you're reading it right now.

So welcome to the SMA gang. You're in now!

If you haven't heard the podcast, don't worry about it. You don't need to – you can still enjoy this book. (A bit weird that you would BUY this book and not bother listening to the FREE podcast, but hey ho, thanks anyway!)

So let's start at the top for all the new kids at the back . . .

We are a 33-year-old married couple with a child. We live in the North East of England and (among other things) we co-host a podcast . . . just as we have co-written this book.

Those other things include:

Rosie: Instagrammer, singer, actor, presenter . . . jack of all trades, master of about four.

Chris: Stand-up comic, presenter, Lego builder and best celebrity dancer north of Wetherby Services.

And obviously both: Podcasters and best-selling authors. ('Best-selling' not actually confirmed yet, so maybe quickly buy another copy of this for your mate or something? Thanks.)

We will each take the lead on different subjects and chapters in this book and the other will butt in whenever they feel like it. Just like real life.

Chris will be in THIS font – Hi!

And Rosie is in THIS font – Hello!

Hopefully it will make sense as you go . . . and you know for a fact you'll all be reading it in our accents in your head as we argue in print form . . . so have fun with that!

So, whoever you are, wherever you are, we hope you enjoy this book.

Whether you are Shagged, Married, Annoyed or all three, thanks for coming.

Have fun.

Shagged

Saturday Nights: Getting Ready

This chapter is called 'Saturday Nights: Getting Ready', but I feel it should be renamed 'Thursday, Friday, Saturday, Sunday, Sometimes Even a Wednesday at the Beginning of the Month Nights: Getting Ready'.

In my late teens and early twenties I could easily bash out four nights on the lash, EASY. I could – and more often than not, did – function quite happily on less than four hours' sleep a night. How did I do that?

Fast-forward to 33 years old and I struggle to go on one night out a month, let alone four a week. Not only because I can't deal with the hangover the next day, but it's so bloody difficult trying to get all my friends together on one night. Plus, there's always someone's fucking kid who's ill.

I'm going to take you back to the good old days right now. It's a Saturday night in 2003. You're in my bedroom which I share with my older sister Kate. It's in my mam and dad's three-bed semi in South Shields.

The room is an average double-sized room at the front of the house. The walls are painted in a magnolia-type colour. We weren't old enough to understand the lushness of a lamp just yet so we lived in big-light hell most of the time. My sister has put a rope across the floor of the room to divide us as much as possible. I say rope, it's more of a really thick piece of string. Like something you would tie around a Christmas present if you wanted to show off. I have no idea where she got it from.

Her side of the room is pristine, as per. My side of the room is a mess, as per.

Genuinely considering employing this in our house now . . .

There are two single beds. Hers is neatly made with a crocheted blanket covering the bottom half; there are three little floral-patterned pillows on her actual sleeping pillow, and Charlie her stuffed monkey sits on top. Pretty weird considering she's 20 and has a full-blown, real-life, grown-up boyfriend with a car who she SPOILER ALERT ends up marrying and having kids with two years later.

The beds used to be bunk beds but due to one of us graffitiing and writing vulgar things about the other on the underneath slats of the bottom bunk, Sandra (my mam) and Kate both decided it would be better to separate them, thus saving themselves from any further graffitiing incidents.

The culprit is still unknown to this very day.

(It was me!! Ssshhhhh . . .)

Another reason for the necessary bed separation is there was this one night when one of us drank a little too much and accidentally vomited over the side of the top bunk, missing the other one who was sleeping peacefully below by mere inches.

It was just a little bit of splashback, honestly not that big of a deal, but anyway, they were separated soon after.

Hold on . . . Your dad (or let's be honest, it was probably Sandra) sawed the bunk beds in two and made two separate single beds?! Were they safe? Were they the same height from the floor? OR were they originally two single beds and the craftsmanship actually came when someone put them on top of each other like the sofa Emmet makes in *The Lego Movie*?! Then they were just separated again to make two singles?! I NEED TO KNOW, ROSIE!

Most bunk beds can be separated. Sandra and Derek were obviously having a flush month and decided to splash out on decent beds, or they bought them on credit. You would never have to know this as you were an extremely lucky 'lonely child' and never had to share a room, let alone a bunk bed. Our beds were separated into single beds and put back together as bunks on several occasions over many years.

Above my now single bed are hundreds of Polaroid pictures of me and my friends. Some old cinema tickets (no idea why) and a calendar which my nana bought me for Christmas and I had yet to write a single entry in. It was also three months behind, much to my sister's annoyance.

Above my sister's bed is a poster of a foot. I know that sounds really ridiculous, but it wasn't a picture of some random person's foot; it was in fact a medical drawing of the sole of a foot, with explanations of each area and how it connected to a part of the human body. Kate was studying to be a reflexologist at the time, so every day I would find myself staring at this picture of a foot above my sister's bed and wonder how the hell we were even related.

She also had a couple of dream catchers along with Charlie,

the stuffed monkey. Kate had had Charlie since she was born. She was really good at looking after stuff so he was pretty much still in mint condition.

Charlie was about the size of a baby orang-utan. He had black fur and a dark brown and orange stomach. His mouth was stitched into a smile and his eyes were beady and sweet. He was a very cute little monkey teddy. On the side of Charlie's stomach there was a small zip and when you opened it, inside there was a little pocket that you could put stuff in.

Ahhh, you're thinking, how lush! He sounds like the best teddy ever! I bet your sister put such cool, quirky little things in there!!

Nope.

Of all the things my sister could have put in there throughout her life – you know, hair bobbles, little letters to herself, sweets . . . So many things she could have chosen!

She chose to put the blue, see-through, unwashed nightgown our mother wore the day she gave birth to each of us in there.

So fucking weird.

It must have been washed since she had you both?! Jesus.

Don't forget Kevin too. Three labours that nightgown lived through.

Anyway, I've totally gone off piste, sorry. Where was I?

Oh yes, now picture this if you will . . .

It's a cold November night in 2003. I'm 17, getting ready for a night out in South Shields.

I wonder how many of you can relate to this.

5:30 p.m.

Ram some food down your neck. Nothing fancy, just something stodgy to soak up the alcohol that was about to
be consumed. Absolute bonus if your mam has made a tea.
Winner!

Have a glass of milk. (No idea why I used to do this. Someone once told me it stopped you from being sick, so I did it
religiously every night before I went out. It never worked. I
don't even like milk.)

Yep. I heard the same rumour. 'It lines your stomach!' they all
said. To the point where our drink of choice for a while in my
friend's house was Malibu and milk. Honest.

6 p.m.

Quick shower or a wash of your nethers over the toilet
with the family jug. We called this a 'Victorian wash' in our
family.

The wash you have depends on how invested you are in
the night out ahead, to be honest. A prearranged close friend
or family member's party warrants a full bath or shower,
whereas a night round the pubs possibly resulting in a
club gets a Victorian wash. I wouldn't dream of doing it
now. I didn't sweat much then and I never really noticed
any sort of odour. Does that come with age, do you think?
(Lie. That's a blatant lie. I definitely would do it now,
sorry.)

Destiny's Child is blasting from the CD player I share
with my sister, getting me in the mood. There were no iPods,

phones or Alexas back then, people! It was all proper Old School.

Make sure to tell whoever is in the house with you to keep an ear out for the door. Your mates will be coming round soon and they'll more than likely be dressed in hardly anything, and you don't need an 18-year-old with hypothermia on your mind, Dad. Not tonight anyway.

Try not to disturb your little brother Kevin because he'll only come sniffing around your mates, and nobody wants to see that. Especially me. No thank you.

Also, remember to shut his bedroom door before they come. It smells like someone has died in there.

I don't think I've ever related to anything less in my entire life. And the idea of the 'family jug' is giving me a panic attack.

6:15 p.m.
Lasses arrive!! Wooooo-hoo!! Lambrini in hand. We are ready to PARTY!

Sandra comes in to say her hellos, as usual.

'Eeeeh, girls, please be careful. It's blowing a frigging hooley out there, mind! Do you need a straw, babe??'

She's always been extremely hospitable has our Sandra, bless her.

6:30 p.m.
Whack some make-up on. Nothing fancy, just a bit of mascara and blusher. If you're lucky your friend might do your eyeshadow for you and curl your hair.

Make-up is so much more complicated these days compared to when I was younger. I really don't want to sound old and out of touch, I'm not even saying that it's a bad thing, I'm just saying it must take an age for young girls now to put it all on.

Also, their clothes must be covered in marks. Imagine hugging one of those lasses who has tons of make-up on? Goodbye clean shoulder, hello rubbed-off foundation . . .

Unfortunately, fake tan wasn't really a thing back in 2003, so unless it was August we were usually all rocking the pale and interesting look.

Oh, and natural hair colours!!!! EW!

7 p.m.

Two bottles of Lambrini and a Babycham (from Sandra) later, it's time fooooorrrrr . . .

'Beg your dad for a lift' time! YEY!! My favourite time of the night!! Not.

'Daaaad . . .'

'Rosie, I've had a can, man!'

'Dad . . . please???!?! I've got no money for a taxi and it's freeeeeeeeezing!!! The bus stop's miles away!!'

'Rosie, why do you have to do this every sodding week? Sandra? She's asking for a frigging* lift again!'

*Frigging was said a lot in my house. I could tell that my parents were DESPERATE to say fucking, but they never ever did. I have a lot of respect for them for that. I mean, it did fuck all as I swear all the time now, but, you know, strong effort, guys.

13

7:15 p.m.

Dad said no.

Bus it is.

The walk to the bus stop was always pretty grim. Goose-bumps as big as a breastfeeding nipple. All of us struggling to walk in our three-inch heels (amateurs).

The fresh air would hit your young, inexperienced liver like a ton of bricks and one of you would inevitably stack it before reaching the actual bus stop.

'One to South Shields, please.'

'That'll be 75p, petal.'

Seventy-five pence. Seventy-five pence for a one-way ticket to good-time city!

To be honest, I always quite enjoyed the bus downtown. It was a safe place. Our time to be able to plan the night ahead of us.

Which bars are we hitting? Who's going to be where? Do you think we'll see such-and-such? Did you know he fingered her last week? OMG! That kind of stuff.

Aaaaah, memories.

Wow.

7:30 p.m.

I just want to take a second to acknowledge the time here: 7:30 p.m.

Back then nights started at a reasonable hour. None of this let's drink in the house and go out at 11 p.m. nonsense. NO. Why? Why are you all doing this now?

Have you walked into a bar at 9 p.m. recently? It's awful! Unless you're in a big city they're 8/10 times bound to be absolutely DEAD. Dead as a nun's chuff. It's soul-destroying and it makes me sad. I did not spend £40 on a new frock from ASOS to only be seen by three people, and that's usually just the bored bar staff.

I crave those busy early night days. Clubs would stop serving at 1:30 a.m. so you would have enough time for some chips and garlic sauce before bundling in a taxi and getting up for work at seven.

I have a 4-year-old now. I can't be out all hours of the night, praying to God that it gets a bit busier before midnight. I would just like a little bit of atmosphere, people! Is that too much to ask for?

7:30 p.m. (It's still only 7:30 . . .)
First bar – FISHBOWLS!* There was literally zero alcohol in these, I swear, but we lapped 'em up! Three pounds each, job's a good'un!

*For those of you who have never experienced a fishbowl, I'll just describe it quickly to you now . . . Imagine a large, see-through Perspex bowl. It's not fancy, it's probably not been washed, to be honest. It has scratches all over it due to years of constant use, so it's no longer see-through but cloudy.

It is filled with shots of all sorts. Vodka, gin, rum, Pernod. Anything you want.

It is then filled with a mixture of fruit juices, making it go a disgusting vomit-like colour, usually a purpley green. Sometimes they would add milk, which would curdle. This was genuinely a thing that people asked for. Not me though, nope – already had me glass of milk, hadn't I?

Smart.

They would then add copious amounts of ice so as to firstly fill up the bowl and secondly sober up the many – let's be honest here – under-age drinkers who were about to consume them.

Everyone would grab a straw and suck away! Beautiful!

They would vary in price. The most expensive one I ever partook in was £25 and it went between around thirty of us so it was proper good value for money, to be fair.

Fishbowls are probably still going somewhere in England, but I personally haven't come across one for about ten years. I might make one at the weekend. Why not, eh? Watch this space . . .

I genuinely think that the rise in people getting spiked on nights out put a stop to the classic fishbowl . . . people ruin everything! I'm going to invent a bowl with a spike-proof mesh or lid over the top, with up to ten straw holes around the side. (Copyright Chris Ramsey Ltd 2020)

8 p.m.

No messing about – we're straight on to the next bar.

It's heaving.

My bones have finally thawed from the cold November night outside.

There are bodies everywhere. Condensation drips down the windows like a scene out of a Britney Spears music video. I am absolutely buzzing.

I'm at the bar having my arse slapped by my mate while we're dancing to *NSYNC's latest banger.

This. Is. Class.

A round of orange Reefs and we are on FIRE!

Literally everyone from college is out.

My friend has just necked on with a randomer and she's now raging as he's rank and is kissing someone else on the other side of the bar.

My other friend is crying in the toilets because her boyfriend won't come and meet her.

I'm dancing like I'm in a music video. The tunes are amazing.

This is class.

I'm 17, in a bar, dancing and drinking. Check me out, man.

I fall down the massive set of stairs on my way out. Everyone sees from downstairs, but nobody really takes much notice as those stairs are lethal and almost every other person falls down them on a nightly basis. They should probably get them redone, to be fair.

9 p.m.

We make our way to the 'shot bar'. I don't know if this is a thing where you grew up, but in my home town there used to be a bar called Pukka Bar where all shots were 50p.

How they ever made any money I have no idea.

My next-door neighbour's son worked on the door so he always let us in, even though my friend Angela is well under age. She was large chested from a young age and could walk really well in high shoes, so she always managed to fool the bouncers. Often better than I could.

I'd have a little catch-up with him, be horrified when he'd run off and manhandle someone down the stairs, down a couple of shots of rum and we're back on our way.

RUM!? Are you a 50-year-old sailor?

Fun fact, a mate of mine once went into Pukka, put £20 on the bar, got forty shots, drank them then had to go to hospital. Fucking idiot.

9:30 p.m.

The drink jacket has well and truly kicked in now. Can't feel a thing. If anything, I'm a bit hot.

10 p.m.

Clubbing time.

I know what you're thinking – 10 p.m.? Bit early for clubbing, isn't it? Yes, you're right. It is extremely early for clubbing.

I have no idea why we went this early. We weren't the only ones in there, it's already really busy! Everyone else has the same idea.

They've got a special offer on – all drinks are two for one before 11!

Aaaaah, that's why we went there so early.

Actually. On the rare occasion that I got into this club, it was because I got there at about 9 p.m. when the doormen weren't there. Rosie isn't aware of this because all girls used to get into all bars and clubs all the time regardless of age, because the doormen were absolute fucking fascist, sexist perverts and can you tell I'm still really angry about it even to this day?!

I've got one word for you, Chris . . . boobs.

10:30 p.m.
We're a few blue WKDs in and the DJ is playing some of the best mega mixes I've heard to date. He's genuinely really talented. He isn't very good in bed, however, so I heard from one of the girls on my course.

11 p.m.
We've walked round the club at least twenty-five times.

There's nothing wrong with us, this is just what we used to do.

There's three sets of stairs in this place and we've had to queue on each of them at least twice as everyone else seems to be walking round the club too.

No wonder I was so bloody thin! Imagine if I'd have had my Fitbit then!

11:30 p.m.
Quick catch-up with an old school friend in the bogs before we hit the dance floor. Oh, hang on, one more walk round just for good luck.

11:40 p.m.
Handbags on the floor, let's dance.

19

The one old man (possibly only 45 but to me at that time he was old AF and disgusting) tries to dance with us.

'I've got a boyfriend. Can you fuck off?'

Liar, you don't have a boyfriend.

It baffles me sometimes that mothers used to worry about girls meeting older men on nights out.

I avoided them like the plague. In fact, I think everyone did. I can remember seeing them flit from one group of young girls to the next, each time being batted down yet still going back for more. You have to give them credit for their efforts. They were always on their own. Perverts don't have many friends, I guess. He could probably cover a lot more ground on his own, to be fair.

Can I just say that as a man of 33 now, the idea of going any-where near a younger group of girls on a night out and dancing or attempting to talk to them scares me so much that I just think this bloke should be commended for his efforts. HOW CONFI-DENT DO YOU HAVE TO BE, MAN!?

No, I was all about the boys my age, thank you! Preferably good-looking ones with nice little six-packs who used too much Lynx. That's my bag.

Here's a little fact for you . . .

Chris and I often used to see each other while out clubbing as we went to the same college. Unfortunately we never hit it off romantically back then. It's a shame, but I'm glad we didn't officially meet until we were a little older and wiser.

You kidding?! You were never stood still long enough to have a conversation with! I can literally remember seeing you come past every fifteen minutes like a slag comet orbiting the DJ booth.

12 a.m.
Disco nap.*

*A disco nap is when you have a little power nap either on or over a club toilet. I used to have these all the time when I was younger – that's probably how I managed to get up for work/college the next day. Mystery solved!

This is tragic. Go home, you mess.

12:30 a.m.
Another toilet chat with a different school friend who you feel like you haven't seen in FOREVER. It's been a couple of weeks at the most.

You spot your cousin and get buzzing that you're both out on the same night, even though it happens almost every weekend.

12:40 a.m.
Quick chat to the lady who gives out the deodorant and chewing gum in the toilets in return for tips. God, love those ladies. How they can stand there all night and watch drunken, moronic girls talk utter shite is beyond me. They deserve a bloody medal!

1 a.m.

More dancing.

A possible sloppy neck-on with your current crush.

Back to dancing.

Avoid the creep.

1:45 a.m.

I'm drunk.

Not the good drunk but the I need to sit down, the room is spinning, I'm hiccuping sick and swallowing it back down my throat drunk. My friends are all drunk too. We decide that now is a good time to go home.

We make our way to the takeaway at the top of Fowler Street. One of us is crying so we all link arms and tell her why her boyfriend is a twat and how she should dump him.

She won't, we never do.

The takeaway is heaving, it's always heaving. It's like an extension of the night! I love it. I order my chips and garlic sauce (I was never a kebab fan and pizzas took too long).

My particular purchase from this establishment was an onion bhaji . . . that's right, this place did the lot! Pizza, chips, burger, curry! It was two for £3 and me and my mate used to walk home eating them like apples. Farts the next day were SOMETHING ELSE!

We decide to walk home because we're irresponsible and the buses have stopped, plus back in the day none of us could afford taxis. They were a total luxury. Wow, my steps on the

Fitbit would have been through the roof! AGAIN, this is how I was so thin.

We stop off for a wee and a cigarette in the local park (sorry, Mam, I know you hate smoking).

The urinating part was never intentional but when you gotta go you gotta go. It eventually became a bit of a ritual. Couldn't not end the night with a wee in the park. I'd often still see the little lines of it while I was walking to college the next morning. Unfortunately, due to my Bambi-like, alcohol-induced state I almost always weed on my feet. Honestly, I dread to think what my shoes must have smelt like.

So easy to wee in public as a bloke that I regularly get annoyed that it's illegal. We can get it into a can, a bottle, a drain, someone's letterbox . . . anywhere!

After the wee and cigarette it was bedtime.

I had to be deathly quiet so as not to wake Kate up. God forbid you wake Queen Kate, Mrs Foot Fetish, goody two shoes, from her slumbers.

One night when I got home having gone a little too hard on the two-for-ones at the club, I somehow ended up with the hallway radiator cover on top of me, waking my parents and siblings in the process.

I don't remember this at all, but my parents assure me that it's true. They said they thought they were being robbed and panic-stricken ran down the stairs, only to find me half-cut lying on the floor with the radiator cover on top of me.

My sister tutted, my brother laughed, my dad helped me up and my mam muttered profanities under her breath and went straight back to bed.

For the record, I could have really hurt myself.

My drunken returns home used to almost always end in me being sick somewhere in my mam and dad's house. If they were lucky it was the toilet, slightly less lucky if it was the bathroom floor, bad luck if it was down the side of my bed, and once I opened my bedroom window and was sick on to the roof of the dining room . . . so glad it was an extension and not a conservatory. Imagine seeing that the next morning when you're having a cuppa. I did have to get up on the roof the next day and hose it down though. That was a bad day.

Night out in 2020, post kids.
    Nice top and jeans.
    Food.
    Wine.
    Bed.
    The end.

I feel it's my duty here to elaborate on just how different mine and Rosie's memories of nights out at this age were.

When I was in college, at 16 and 17 years old, everyone started going out on the lash of a night. The days of hanging about the street on your bike or playing football in the park quickly disappeared, and the days of talking about how amazing and mental and class last night was were here.

Some lads I knew started going out to pubs and clubs WHEN WE WERE STILL AT SCHOOL! Unbelievable, I know. A lad called Jamie once came into GCSE English HUNG-OVER! Telling tales of places he'd been the night before with such exotic names as 'Evissa', 'Coast' and 'Vogue'.

I couldn't believe it. We were kids. And he has been out . . . CLUBBING! I say kids – him and the other lads he went with hadn't looked like kids since we were in Year 8. You know the kind of lads I mean – had a beard since he was nine and a full set of pubes since he was three. The lads who answered to their name during the class register with a deep, booming 'YES, SIR' that sounded like builders backing up in a cement truck. The kind of lads who squared up to the teachers in Year 11 rather than take the telling off.

Cunts. The word I'm looking for is cunts. Fast developers who left the puny, weak, smooth-tiddlered Chris Ramseys of the world in their uber-masculine dust.

(Just on the subject of pubes, lads . . . how utterly terrifying was it when you spotted the first lad in your PE class to get his pubes?! There is no greater feeling of devastation and inadequacy in this world. It's the ultimate FOMO. Your crotch is as pure as the driven snow and a lad who is supposed to be the same age as you looks like he's wet his genitals and rolled on a barber shop floor. It's not fair. You imagine word will get out and everyone will know he has hairy man balls and you are a pubeless wonder. All the girls will fancy him and you'll die alone. Genuinely, I once had a girlfriend when I was 12 and a bigger boy said to her, 'Do you like hairy armpits?', while rolling up the sleeves of his Newcastle away shirt to show off said armpits, and she said YES. Right in front of me. I knew right there and then that she was probably not marriage material . . . she'd probably ditch me at the altar if the driver taking her to the church had a thick mane of jet-black arse-crack hair she could get hold of.)

Ew.

Anyway . . . nights out.

I never regularly got served in pubs until I was 18. Literally the day of my eighteenth birthday was the day I stopped getting asked for ID by bouncers. Infuriating. I was an August baby too, so my eighteenth birthday came just before most of my mates' nineteenth birthdays . . . and they had already been getting into the clubs since they were 16.

I had a beautiful collection of fake IDs ordered from the back of *FHM* that did get me through the doors now and then. A national identity card, fake student card and one particular card that a bunch of lads managed to convince every doorman in South Shields was a Fire Brigades Union card. We got in for a while, but the entire place would have been fucked if a fire started and they called on us to help. We'd have probably just thrown glasses of Vodka Red Bull on it and burnt the whole place down.

So my memories of 'Saturday Nights Getting Ready' are very different from Rosie's. While hers may have been excitement and doing each other's make-up, mine were nerve-wracking and worrying. I genuinely used to get ready at home, and before taking my carrier bag of cans (or bottle of milk) to my mate's house, I would march around the house, trying on all manner of shirts and trousers while repeatedly asking my mam, 'Do I look eighteen, Mam?'

'You look lovely, son!'

'That's very nice of you to say, Mam, BUT DO I LOOK EIGHT-EEN?!'

Tragic this like, Chris.

I don't think I looked particularly young, to be honest, not when I was 16 or 17. I knew lads who were smaller and younger than me who got in all the time . . . I think I just had a shit poker face.

I must have walked up to those doors looking like I was literally filling my pants with shit. Terrified of the big bald men either side who held the key to your night's success in the palm of their giant meat shovel of a hand.

There was nothing like the castrating feeling of getting knocked back from a bar that all of your mates from college AND the girl you fancied were inside of, having a brilliant time . . . probably shagging on the dance floor by now. I bet it's brilliant. And here's me in a back lane swapping shirts with my mate and getting up the courage to try again.

We would swap shirts, jackets, shoes, pants – the lot. Once a club were absolutely FINE with our age, they just said we needed shoes not trainers . . . so we went in the back lane, put our black socks OVER OUR TRAINERS and went in. Unbeliev-able. They looked like Teletubby feet.

I cannot believe that this actually ever happened. Those door-men must have had a right laugh that night.

Not that I regularly wore trainers, to be honest. I had it in my head that black dress shoes, black dress trousers and a black pinstripe shirt with white collar and cuffs made me look older, so that was my regular going out attire. No wonder I kept getting knocked back. I must have looked like I was in fucking *Bugsy Malone*.

We would try everything to get in. Sometimes someone who was already in would open the fire escape for you. People used to say, 'Walk in with a girl and you'll get in', which, considering I didn't know any girls and was out to specifically meet girls, always seemed a bit harsh.

Another rumour was that if you were smoking, you looked older. (You could smoke in pubs then. How old do we all feel now, eh? Can we just take a moment to talk about how much your pillow ABSOLUTELY STANK the next morning after a night out? Like it had been used to douse a bonfire. Horrific . . . although, sneaky casual smoker Rosie probably woke up and sucked on her pillow to get a little hint of tobacco. Minger!)

Those were the days . . .

I remember walking up towards a pub, and seeing doormen on it, a guy we were with said, 'I don't have any ID', so one lad handed him a lit cigarette and said, 'Hold that, it'll make you look older.' He replied, 'But I don't smoke.' 'JUST HOLD IT!'

So he did. He attempted to walk past the doormen with his arm outstretched in front of him, with his middle and index finger pointing to the sky and his brand-new cigarette (his first one ever) wedged between his skyward fingers. He looked like a fucking idiot. It looked a bit like the cigarette had him under some kind of spell and was controlling his body from his hand. And get this, he got halfway in, had to turn slightly to let someone out and ended up burning a hole in the doorman's jacket. Needless to say, he held the rest of his cigarette outside in the car park.

Yes, mine and Rosie's nights out were very different back then – hers full of anticipation and excitement, mine wracked with fear and self-loathing ... then when I started getting in places, they kind of just become a bit of a blur.

One-Night Stands . . .

```
What exactly do you think constitutes a one-
night stand?

Have both of you ever had one?

I'm 22 and I've never had one yet.

Anon
```

In my opinion, a one-night stand is when you meet someone whom you have never met before in your life. You have no idea who they are, they are a complete stranger to you. You have sex with them once, then you never see them again.

Chris agrees.

Oh, apparently I agree, guys! I've been told I agree, so there we go. No need for me to type anything here. Or anywhere else for that matter? Let's just let Rosie decide what I'm thinking on all of these things. I'll just stay quiet, shall I?

Annoyingly, I do agree. You can't have a one-night stand with someone you know . . . that's just having sex with someone you know. And if you see a stranger again after a one-night stand, it's not one night any more. So yeah. Nailed it.

You're wasting our time, Chris.

Gotta get that word count up!

True.

Very important, that word count!

I agree.

I also agree, Rosie, I also agree.

Me too, Christopher, me too.

I personally find one-night stands soooo interesting.

You see, some people have had loads. Amazing, why the hell not? As long as you're careful and no one is getting hurt, GO FOR IT! Just, you know, make sure you put something on the end of it . . . Jezza Kyle style.

A lot of people – like yourself, anon – have never had a one-night stand in their lives. Not one!

I still can't decide whether I pity or envy you/them, to be honest.

There must be something pretty gratifying about knowing that you have enough self-control to not give in to your sexual demons. You have the ability to control your animal instincts, and two bottles of wine and three shots of Jäger don't tip you over the edge into one-night-stand land.

You can say no to a bar of chocolate at the checkout tills. You never snooze your alarm. You say yes to an invitation and by jove you'll be there, come hell or high water. No flakiness from you. No sirree. You are in control of your life and I envy you. There, look, I've made up my mind. I envy you.

You wouldn't dream of jumping into bed with someone who you've only known for thirty minutes. Don't get me wrong – you're not a prude, you just like to have been on a date, exchanged a few texts, etc., before you do 'the deed'.

Good for you, I say! You've got morals and you stick by them. The world needs more people like you.

So, you've got your prolific one-night standers, every weekend there's a different person in their bed, not ashamed in the slightest, couldn't give a fuck (or quite the opposite . . . they've got fucks going spare!).

Then you've got your holier-than-thou wouldn't even dream of it types, couldn't possibly imagine kissing a stranger, let alone have sex with one.

Then you have people like me, bobbing somewhere in-between.

I was a typical on the fencer. I had all the makings of a non-one-night stander but unfortunately too many break-ups and my need to be loved (tragic but true) let me down.

Sending hugs!

I can also confidently say 'was' because I am now thankfully happily married. (I'm married to the other person writing this book. Luckily we're extremely open about everything and he doesn't mind hearing about my past relationships. Imagine if he did? You'd not be reading this right now, that's for sure.)

Still, though, I'd be lying if I said I wasn't slightly nervous to read on . . .

Anyway, this was very much me for most of my twenties. The sex was mostly rebound sex, to be honest, and I never felt good after it – the complete opposite, actually.

Ah, that's OK then.

I'm not sure whether that's a personal thing or a female thing.

A lot may disagree with me here, but I think it's a lot easier for a man to have a one-night stand than a woman.

I don't know about that, but it's definitely a lot easier for a woman to HAVE a one-night stand than a man, like, to actually initiate one. Single blokes on nights out are so desperate that most women could get the DJ to do a shoutout for them and there would be a queue of guys to pick from.

Men are very much in, out, job's a good'n, never need to think of them again.

Not us. Oh no, no, no, no. Us ladies, we dwell on this sort of shit for days, weeks sometimes. Who am I kidding? I'm sat here ten years later still kicking myself about a one-night stand.

'Ah God. Why the fuck did I sleep with that guy? I didn't even know him! Seriously, are you that lonely, Rosie? You don't even know his surname. You absolute whore bag. What if you see him again and he doesn't even remember you? Nah, he'd remember you . . . Right? You looked nice last night and you'd done your bikini line, thank God!'

He got you on a good night, babes. Lucky bastard if you ask me. #selflove

Should I find him on Facebook? No. That's awful. Complete cringe. He didn't ask for my number so why would he want me to find him on Facebook? That whole aloof, playing it cool thing you did this morning, Rosie, did you absolutely no favours and was way too convincing. I doubt he's even bothered about seeing you again.

Ah Christ, I said some well raunchy stuff last night. He genuinely got some of my best flipping moves. You could tell it'd been a while, babe, you went all out!

Ah God, the utter SHAME of it all!

What if I see him in Tesco? What if he works somewhere I go and I've just not noticed? What if our children end up going to school together?? They'd have to leave! Imagine!!

What if I end up working with his mam/sister/auntie (insert any known relative here)? I can't go on like this! I need some answers!!

OK, well, look. If it's going to make you stop going on about it, just have a quick look. It won't harm anyone. He might have already messaged you, you never know! He might be doing exactly the same thing right now! Oh my God. Imagine if this is your future husband?? Shit the bed, he could be the one. What the fuck is his fucking surname? Aaaaaahhh!

He hasn't messaged.

Fuck.

This is down to you. Just look, he won't even know . . .

OK, so he knows whatshisface who works at the pub. Find him, you're friends with him.

He might be on there.

Right. John. His name was definitely John.

John, John, John . . . Where the hell are you, John?

Friends list . . . Nope. Comments section . . . Nope. Tagged pics . . . BINGO! There you are!!!

Aaaah, you're actually really sweet-looking! Yey! Eeeeeeh, this is actually quite exciting! He was good in bed too! Tick! Eeek! This could be it!!!

Clicks on to profile

Heart racing. Hands sweating.

This is ridiculously exciting, isn't it? I literally left this guy's house just three hours ago knowing zero about him other than his first name and that he's friends with that random lad who works weekends in the pub.

But he was nine-wines-in fit and he was good in bed, so let's just see, eh??

Hang on.

Is that . . . ?

No, no, it can't be.

I can't frigging see on this little flipping screen!!

Zooms in

That's better. There we go.

Is that . . . ?

Is that a girl in his profile pic? EH?

It could be his sister? Or maybe his mam is really young-looking?

Just a second.

People kiss their sisters, right?
On the lips, in an embrace . . . right?
Nope. No, they don't.
You utter mug.
Legit girlfriend.
Ah, John.
You absolute wanker.

I almost had a panic attack reading that! What an emotional rollercoaster. Did this happen? Is John real? The people need to know, Rosie!

He is absolutely real but I changed his name for legal reasons. Prick.

I can honestly say I think I might have only ever had one one-night stand . . . possibly two. I think all others I either knew beforehand in some way, shape or form, or we ended up going out again in the future . . . one of them even hung around like a bad smell long enough to get married, have kids and do a bloody podcast together!

You're welcome.

I feel strange, as a bloke, having to talk about one-night stands here . . . with my wife (and who knows how many other people) reading it. I can definitely say that I DESPERATELY wanted to be that one-night stand 'legend' when I was younger. The guy who just 'pulls' on a night out then is out the following night looking for a different girl . . . what a hero he was! But it's not until you're older when you think . . . oh, he was a bit of a prick, wasn't he?

Yes.

I remember once being out with my mates on a Saturday night, and one of them had slept with a girl on the Friday, so, less than twenty-four hours ago. I was standing with him, and the girl he had slept with was literally about fifteen feet away. I spotted her and said, 'There's the girl you got with last night, are you going to go and talk to her?' He said no. He just went on with his night, as did she. They never really paid any attention to each other and left with different people at the end of the night. I realized then that I am NOT THAT GUY. Come on! You were literally inside that person half a day ago and you're not even going to say hello? I'd have gone up and asked for a review at least.

'Hi, it's me, Chris from last night. As part of my after-BUCK service I'd just like you to take a quick survey to help improve my bucking in the future.'

I do have one LEGENDARY one-night stand story that I can tell you which was epic . . .

I was out and ended up going back to university halls with a girl and the one-night stand happened.

Fucking hell, Chris, it's called sex. You're a 33-year-old man – you are allowed to say sex.

My phone had run out of battery and she didn't have an iPhone (it would have never lasted) so I had no idea what time it was when I left. I was walking along hoping to flag down a taxi when I spotted a McDonald's. I went in and asked for a Big Mac Meal. I don't massively love McDonald's the way Rosie does. I will eat a Big Mac now and then, but I do LOVE the breakfasts. The guy behind the counter looked at me with some confusion and said, 'Sorry, mate, it's 5:30 a.m. We're serving breakfast now.' So I got a Sausage and Egg McMuffin meal instead. ABSO-LUTE LEGEND!

Ghosting

For those of us over 30, we should probably explain what 'ghosting' actually means . . . because we had absolutely no idea and genuinely had to google it when a question from the public on it came in. It sounded like something from an episode of *Scooby-Doo* to us.

Here it is for all us old fuckers:

Ghosting Definition

The practice of ending a personal relationship with someone by suddenly and without explanation withdrawing from all communication.
   Oxford English Dictionary

It's basically the modern version of 'Your Da went to the shops for a packet of cigarettes and never came home . . .'

Now that I know what it means I can safely say that yes, I have definitely been ghosted.

A few times actually.

How rude! To just up and leave someone's life without a simple explanation or a goodbye. I find it all very odd, to be honest.

Chris, have you ever ghosted anyone? Or been ghosted

yourself? You'd probably not even notice if someone ghosted you, to be fair.

Well, until I looked up that definition I had no idea what ghosting was either. Well, I did have an idea, but it was completely wrong. I thought ghosting was when you do a poo then wipe and there's nothing on the paper ... but that's probably for another chapter.

Dear God, I hope not.

I'm going to sound like such a miserable prick here, but I genuinely think that I'd absolutely LOVE to be ghosted by easily half the people I know. It would be amazing not to hear from shitloads of them ever again ... I'm not talking about close mates here, mainly people who keep adding me to their bloody LinkedIn profiles and people who have your personal email address (because you know them) but then they add you to their work newsletter too, like I was interested in their new venture in the first place?!

'Oh, you've started an online yoga class, have you? WELL DONE! I only emailed you that one time to organize a mutual friend's surprise party! I don't want to be kept up to date with your expanding wellness business! If you want to play that game, mate, I'll get you signed up to every single messed-up porn site I can find ... I've got a VPN and private browsing enabled on my laptop, I'm not scared. Let's dance!'

Anyway, sadly, I don't think I have ever been ghosted ... not because I'm sat here thinking I'm too cool to be ghosted, or that people need me in their life or that I'm super popular . . . quite the opposite. I'm such an annoying prick that it would be impossible to ghost me, because of the hundreds of texts I would bombard you with . . .

'Mate? Did you get my text?'

'Reply, you rude twat!'

'I can see the little blue ticks, you've seen my text.'

Sends screen-grab photo of the blue ticks

'SEE!'

'Ah, I see you've just turned read notifications off so it looks like you didn't get those last ones, nice one . . .'

SWITCHES TO WHATSAPP

'Still got them on here though, haven't you?!'

Sends screen-grab photo of the blue ticks

'YES. YES, YOU HAVE.'

'Just seen you posted something on Facebook . . . so . . . that's nice.'

'I'

'will'

'just'

'keep'

'texting'

'until'

'you'

'reply'

'I'm'

'on'

'a'

'train'

'and'

'the'

'wi-fi'

'is'

'free'

This would go on indefinitely until they caved. Ghosting would be out of the question ... It would be easier to just text me telling me to outright fuck off, or give in and be my friend for ever. Consider yourselves all warned. That goes for you too, Rosie, although as we live in the same house, I could probably be a bit more annoying in person. Again, you have been warned.

You are so hard to ghost, Chris. You wouldn't believe the amount of times I've tried to get rid of you around the house, but no, you always keep coming to check on me, see if I'm OK and that I'm 'still your friend' after a heated argument. You are the hardest person to get rid of EVER.

I'll take that as a compliment!

Question is, have I ever ghosted anyone . . . ?

Erm, maybe? I'm honestly not too sure. I've definitely never disappeared off the face of the planet, that's for sure – our home town is way too small for that, unfortunately.

I have definitely not texted someone back as often as I should have, or as much as they have texted me. Missed a few calls here and there? Yes, I'm definitely guilty of that. Whoops. But I don't think it counts as full-blown ghosting . . .

The thing is, in this day and age 'dating' is so different. There's so many bloody forms of communication!

Text
Calls
FaceTime
Emails
WhatsApp
Facebook Messenger
Instagram
Twitter

These are only the ones that I have on my phone! I can guarantee there are more.

Remember when the only way to communicate with a crush was on the house phone? My first boyfriend's parents used to have cable TV with a phone offer that allowed you free evening calls up to one hour long. After 6 p.m. he would call me and we'd sit on the phone for HOURS. We would hang up after an hour, on the hour, then he'd call me back after a few minutes. We were wise to the system and found a way around it. Savvy.

I can remember it so vividly. The phone in my house was an off-white colour with a long, curly cord. It was hung on the kitchen wall next to the door, right next to the dining table and the radiator. Perfectly placed for long, comfortable chats witcha lover (yes, that is supposed to say witcha, a bit like don'tcha).

Imagine living with this.

SH**GED. MARRIED. ANNOYED.

I'd sit there for hours but often I'd leave the phone on the radiator as I went in the bath or had my tea.

Family members would pick it up and be like 'Hello? You still there? She's just in the bath, I'll leave the phone here.' He would be like 'Yep, still here.' Or on the odd occasion he would be having his tea or possibly talking to one of his mates at his front door, while carrying the phone round like he's on hold on a really important call. His phone was cordless, you see, his parents were clearly doing better than mine. Cable AND cordless, pure luxury.

To this day I have absolutely no idea why we didn't just hang up. I think it's because it was free. Love a bargain, me.

Should have just bought a pair of walkie-talkies, you fucking idiots.

It was so random, but that's what we did most nights. Luckily my mam and dad were clearly unpopular AF as they never complained about me hogging the phone line much. The only time they became annoyed was when my boyfriend's parents' cable deal finished and upon receiving the phone bill they realized their daughter's romantic phone dalliances were costing them a small fortune.

Not long after, they decided, much to my siblings' disapproval, that we were all to use the phone box over the road. My dad would watch us out the window to make sure we were 'safe'.

Seriously? How cheap, man! He'd rather waste his evenings watching his teenage kids stand in a freezing-cold phone box than pay for a phone bill?! Cruel.

This is absolutely ridiculous. It must have looked like you were a family of drug dealers to the neighbours, or at the very least, operating some kind of phone phishing scam from there ... Then again, if they knew your family at all, they would assume you just kept nipping out to see if anyone had left any money in the change tray.

After a few weeks of this MADNESS we had a family meeting. We all complained, and my dad (growing wise to the fact that we still had to pay for the phone box across the road) introduced what was essentially an IN-HOUSE PHONE BOX: a little cardboard box with 'phone money' written on the side in big letters. He'd even made a little slot on the side too. He hung said box on the wall in the kitchen next to the phone.

My siblings and I would begrudgingly put our coins in when we wanted to call someone. He'd often walk past while you were on the phone and shake it to check you'd deposited the correct amount of money and then he'd get back to his evenings as Ebenezer Scrooge in front of the telly.

Looking back, it's genius really.

Bravo, Derek, bravo.

Obviously when mobile phones came along, it completely changed the way we lived. Think back now to your first mobile phone. What was it called? How did it look? How did it feel?

Mine was a hand-me-down from my older sister.

Shock. Almost everything I owned had once been owned by my sister. I'm surprised I didn't slowly morph into her the amount of bloody clothes I wore of hers. The ridiculous thing is that she's always been at least a good five inches taller than me our whole lives. The teachers must have been laughing their heads off on my first day of comp when I strutted in looking like a prize prat in my sister's old blazer. It was massive! I never grew into it. By the time I'd reached the correct age it was dropping to bits, so I always just looked like a teeny tiny child wearing an adult's clothes.

Luckily we have always had different-sized feet, so my shoes were always my own. Saving grace.

My sister had been collecting Coca-Cola ring pulls on the sly because pop was only allowed in our house at Christmas and birthdays and never in can form. Christ, we didn't even have proper Coke – it was Rola Cola at best. Jeez, Sandra, you were well strict! It's a wonder we haven't all disowned you!! (I'm joking, obvs. She makes an amazing Sunday roast.)

Fifteen secret, bought-on-the-sly cans of pop later, plus some money she'd saved from her Saturday job, and Kate had saved enough to buy the Coca-Cola mobile phone.

God, I was jealous.

The phone was a Sony Ericsson. It was black with a huge, ugly, poking-out grey aerial. It was designed to look like a cold can of pop just out of the fridge, so it had a silver screen over and around the buttons, with droplets of water printed on it and the Coca-Cola logo.

It was so beautiful.

I used to pretend that it was mine when she wasn't looking. I'd read all of her texts and pretend to accept phone calls. I'd play the ring tone over and over again. It only had one and it was the Coca-Cola tune, proper on brand: 'Doo-doo-do-do-do-do. Always Coca-Cola!'

This is absolutely tragic. I'm embarrassed for you.

It was a pretty shite phone, to be fair. It could only receive and make calls and texts, literally nothing else, but by golly I was desperate for it! And you know what, guys? Dreams do come true . . .

DREAM BIG, ROSIE!

Kate – 'Mam, this phone doesn't really do much. The new Nokia one that Laura's got has games on and stuff. I think I might save up and get one of those instead.'

Mam – 'Ah Kate, that's a shame. You've only just got it, pet. What you going to do with it?'

Kate – 'I'm not sure. I could maybe sell it? Someone might want it. Maybe someone at school?'

Mam – 'Yeah, maybe, love. Can't think of anyone who would need it that we know.'

ARE YOU FUCKING KIDDING ME??? AM I INVISIBLE???

Me (from the other room) – 'I'LL HAVE IIIIIIIIIII-ITTTTTTTT!!!!!!!!!!!'

I swooped in, grabbed the phone from her hand and stuck it down my crotch so that all she could say was, 'Ew, that's disgusting! You can have it.' This may sound dramatic, but if you grew up in a household of three siblings you will under-stand that you often had to stoop to low tactics in order to keep things for yourself.

It was more often than not food-related in our house. My knicker drawer was my special hiding place – it was often filled with packets of crisps and Trio biscuits. Again, I know this sounds dramatic, but in our house if you didn't steal them when they were fresh from the shops then you could bet your bottom dollar that they would be gone by the time 6 p.m. came. We all did it. Even my dad used to stash food away in the garage. I found his stash of Mars bars once and took little bites out of them, and he thought we had mice. Looking back, it really was ridiculous – we were complete gannets! The problem was, Sandra wouldn't buy sweets and crisps very often. We were never one of those families who had a snack cupboard – she was always so strict when it came to what we ate – which is why I now have a sugar addiction. If she'd had a steady supply then I think we'd all have got fed up of sweets and chocolate eventually, it would have become the norm and we wouldn't be forced to steal.

I was so envious of my friends whose houses had a ready supply of ket! (That's Northern slang for sweets – apologies if that makes no sense to you. It's also an abbreviation of the drug ketamine, isn't it? Makes sense in this instance, really, doesn't it?)

I would go to their houses and their parents would offer us a snack, and I'd already be drooling from the mouth at the very thought of a 'proper' bag of crisps. You know, like a branded bag, not the no-frills flavourless shite my mam used to bring home. They had Walkers, Monster Munch, Space Raiders, Chipsticks! It was like living in a dream. We'd have sandwiches with thick white bread and ham in the shape of teddy bears' faces, jelly sweets and chocolate bars all already in the house. Just sat there waiting for us in the cupboard! Heaven, absolute heaven.

I must stress here that my mam isn't an awful woman who wouldn't let us eat anything nice; she's quite the opposite, in fact. The truth is we went through a time in our childhoods where both my parents had to quit work, so all of these items became a luxury. It's made me appreciate things so much more than I might have. I still get excited to go to McDonald's or forage in the fridge for a cheeky Snickers bar, as they just didn't happen often when I was growing up.

Chris won't understand any of this, unfortunately, as I recently discovered that his parents used to give him a packet of crisps and a chocolate bar after every meal. EVERY MEAL. Imagine!

Er, it's called 'dessert', Rosie.

Back to the phone debacle . . .

BOOM! Rosie's got a new phone!!!! (Better give it a quick wipe though.)

School the next day.

Here's my number, bitchez. Call me, drop me a text, let's communicate!

This is the future!!! It doesn't fit in any of my pockets (even on the massive blazer), but I don't give a shit!

HAVE YOU HEARD THE RINGTONE?! I know. Amazing.

Two weeks later . . .

Me to my sister – 'Yeah, it's actually pretty shit, isn't it?'

Kate – 'Yeah.'

Skip forward eighteen years (fucking hell!). Here I am hating the mere sight of my phone. Struggling daily to text any of my friends back, juggling family life with answering emails. Don't even get me started on WhatsApp groups. Literally the bane of my LIFE!

Oh, the perils of being too popular, Rosie! I do feel the same, BUT sometimes I come home and think, 'I'll put my phone on silent and leave it in another room for the afternoon, so no one bothers me . . . I've been on tour, I want to see my family.' I sometimes leave it a whole day, then I go back to it and there is ABSOLUTELY NOTHING! It hurts. It really hurts.

I swear when I hear that ping I get a feeling of dread run through my whole body because I don't have time to reply. I'm struggling to finish a poo properly, let alone read sixty-three messages! Why do people send so many short, separate ones? I'm having to put my phone on silent because you can't be arsed to write in full paragraphs. Are you being attacked?? Are you ill?? This is not OK!

Send me a voice note, please! For the love of God, send me a voice note!

Also, apologies if this sounds at all 'preachy'. It's taken me years to finally realize that time really is precious.

Lovely to hear Rosie showing off about her old boyfriend exhausting his parents' cable phone deal for the hours and hours of romantic chats they would have . . . I myself didn't really have a proper girlfriend until mobile phones were a common thing. So thanks for reminding me of that. I did have a couple of girlfriends, but both were when I was in Year 7. One I started going out with the day we broke up for the Christmas holidays, didn't get her phone number and came back to school after Christmas to discover she had a different boyfriend, so no phone chats there.

The other I did chat to on the phone during the summer holidays but then the paper lad in my street told me that she'd had sex with an older boy in a tent in someone's garden, so that really put an end to the phone calls before we could run up any kind of hefty bill . . . Plus I didn't have cable. Maybe the guy in the tent did? Might have been what she saw in him.

She went to my school! Eeeh, small world.

I do remember getting in trouble for clogging the house phone up when I got dial-up internet. My mam or dad would go to make a call and hear that horrendous sound like a printer having sex with a fax machine screaming from the receiver and shout upstairs for me to come off the internet so they could make a call. Ironically, if they'd just got me cable and a tent I wouldn't have had to be on the internet that much at all.

My first mobile phone was a Maxon MX-3204 in silver. I had no idea that was what it was called – I've only just found out now from an extensive Google session while writing this and I've come face to face with an image of my first phone, and I've got to say, I still quite like it. I'd have it over a Coca-Cola ring-pull phone any day of the week!

Rude.

It was a brick, to be fair, but I loved it.

On my first day of taking it to school a lad called David pushed me off a wall and it dropped out of my pocket and got scratched on the floor. I definitely cried. No lies. After that I got a cover for it which multiplied its brickishness by ten, because when I say 'cover' I don't mean the kind of perfect-fitting, clip-on cases we have for our super-sleek smart phones these days; I mean a leather pouch. Remember them? Leather pouch, Velcro opener at the top, leather over the earpiece so you could hear absolutely fuck all of the person on the other end, clear rubber screen and button protector on the front that went white after too much use and ALWAYS ended up with crumbs in it somehow, and a belt clip on the back that absolutely no one ever used. Ever.

I had one too but I heard that you'd get cancer in your hip so I never used it.

I didn't text girls on it. I didn't text anyone on it. I couldn't afford to. I had one of those shocking early pay-as-you-go plans where you had to put DAYS and CREDIT on it?! Half of a top-up card would go on each. You would check your credit and it would say 'You have £5 and 10 days to use it.' Not a problem, mate, it's about a pound a minute anyway. So by the time I've walked around to my mate's house then whipped it out to call my mam and ask her 'What's for tea?', I'm spent anyway. Utter waste of time. And it didn't even have Snake.

In all my life I don't think I've ever felt jealousy like the first time I saw a lad at school with a Nokia 3210. I'd have strangled him for it.

Bit extreme?

It's got Snake AND when David pushes you off the wall and it gets a scratch you can CHANGE THE FUCKING COVER! Be still, my beating heart. And when the 3310 came out, I genuinely asked my mam to consider home schooling me, so I didn't have to leave the house with my silver brick of disappointment clipped to my school pants. If you could have shown 14-year-old me an iPhone I think he would have ejaculated in his borrowed PE shorts (I often forgot mine), and if you'd then told him that by his thirties he'd be sick of the sight of the thing and literally leave it in another room to sometimes get away from it, he'd have pushed you in a hedge (this was a thing we did on the way home from school a lot).

I never understood why lads did this.

Here's another question from the public about ghosting.

Hi Rosie & Chris,

Recently I've been unlucky in love. Two days before Christmas I was ghosted by my boyfriend of one month. Then six months later I was ghosted by my next boyfriend of four months, two days before my birthday!

Seriously, I thought, when will this end?! Then I was set up on a blind date by my manager. He was lovely. We started dating for a few weeks and it was going well (or so I thought).

This guy knew about the recent ghosting and how much it hurt me. Then after spending a nice weekend together, it ended well and he told me to send him before and after pictures of my eleven-mile run (I'm training for a half-marathon).

Then after sending him a picture after the run, saying I was getting a McDonald's (oops), I didn't hear a thing. I messaged him a week later, he messaged back saying he was busy, we had a short conversation. Then I asked him a question . . . no response. It's now been over a week.

Yet again, I have been ghosted. When will this end?

My question to you two is, is ghosting ever
acceptable? If so, in what situation?

I think if you both ghost each other after
the first date, that's fine. Other than that,
it's just rude. Especially two days before my
birthday and Christmas! (Cheapskates not
wanting to buy a present.)

Kristina

Ah, Kristina my love. Bless your heart! What rotten luck! Unfortunately, I fear that you may turn into an actual ghost by the amount of times you have been ghosted.

I can't believe that you've been unlucky enough to have this happen three times, consecutively too! Maybe the most recent guy is a bit of a dick who doesn't like women who go running and enjoy themselves by eating at McDonald's? Although he did ask you to send him a picture. (That is a bit weird, don't you think?) Maybe he doesn't like fast food? I've heard a rumour that some people don't, you know. Luckily I've never had the misfortune of meeting one myself, but apparently they do exist. I guess unfortunately you're never going to find this out, as they have all quite clearly moved on.

I still can't help but find the whole ghosting thing extremely rude. I mean, a simple text would do. If anything, babe, they've all done you a favour. Nobody needs to be wasting time on a person who doesn't give them the attention they deserve. You need a man who will be desperate to hear from you. You want to be with someone who texts you non-stop, so much so that you have to eventually tell them, 'Whoa! Love! No offence, but BACK THE FUCK OFF!'

That's what you want. And it will happen, though you've got to kiss a lot of frogs before you find your prince. Or in your case, visit a lot of graves . . . (Ghosting. Get it? No? OK, my mistake.)

Two days before Christmas?! Two days before your birthday?! Wow. They are either heartless bastards, or they forgot to get you a present and felt so bad about it, they faked their own disappearance, left their shoes on the beach and disappeared into the sea. And this third bloke just sounds like he hates running AND McDonald's. When you mentioned the run he was like, 'I hate running, my whole family were killed by a run . . . but I like this girl', THEN you threw McDonald's in and he was like, 'WHAT?! They were running TO McDonald's when they all got killed. This is too much!' So, if you can believe that and take some solace from it (even though it's stupid and bollocks) then please do. I reckon he just didn't have as much of a good time that weekend as you did . . . but he probably should have told you! I once got slagged off by an ex for finishing it via text . . . AT LEAST I FINISHED IT! At least there was closure! God, I wish ghosting was a thing then so I could have said all of this.

I think it's always been a thing, babe, it's just got a name now.

When You Gonna Get a Real Job?

I can quite confidently say that I've had loads more jobs than Chris has, so I'm taking the lead on this one.

I started working/grafting when I was 14 years old. Young? Yes, I thought so too.

Looking back it was pretty much slave labour, but Sandra (my mother) insisted that if I wanted any sort of social life then I needed to pay for it myself, as she was only willing to fund the absolute bare essentials of my life.

According to Sandra, the bare essentials were:

- Tampons
- Deodorant
- School uniform
- Dinner
- Weekly pocket money: £2

I actually got £5 a week pocket money but that might have been taking into account the fact that I didn't need as many tampons as you.

Seriously, Sandra? What did you think I would be able to buy with £2? Granted it was only 20p to get on the bus back then, but I used to ride the bus A LOT. Where's my chips money? Where's my Lambrini in the cemetery money? Very unfair.

To quote my mother directly: 'I'm not giving you money to fritter away on McDonald's and daft unnecessary shopping trips with your mates.'

Hurtful but true. I was on large meals by 14 so my £2 didn't go far at the golden arches.

Lies, you were blatantly on Supersize.

I decided to get myself a job at a local ice cream parlour which does the best ice cream I've ever had.

It's run by an Italian family in South Shields. My sister worked at the kiosk on the seafront and I worked in the café in the village. Kate was happy about this arrangement as it meant she didn't have to spend any more time with me than was absolutely necessary. Plenty of distance between us. I would work most nights after school in the ice cream parlour and sweet shop which was attached to the café at the back.

I know what you're thinking. 'Wow! I bet it was amazing working in a sweet shop/ice cream parlour/café when you were 14?' Yes. You're absolutely right. It was fucking brilliant.

I ate so much shite while I worked there I'm surprised they didn't have to wheel me out of the place. Thank God they didn't do regular stock takes as I'd have been sacked on the spot. It was also right next to a fish and chip shop, so you can imagine how much I used to eat.

The pay was pretty terrible at £2.50 per hour, but once I'd

worked all my shifts that week I was minted. Well, minted for a 14-year-old at least.

Working in an ice cream shop at 14?! I'm just jealous because I only had a paper round . . .

Haters gonna hate.

One summer by the end of the holidays, I had a stash of notes. I was like a drug dealer walking round the house, bribing my younger brother to get me glasses of juice from the kitchen for a pound a shot. Absolute boss.

The café isn't actually there any more which I find really sad as the corned beef and onion toasties were to die for. It's a Domino's now, though, so . . . every cloud.

It probably wasn't making enough money and had to shut down because you'd eaten your weight in bonbons every shift!

I'll not tell you every job I've ever had as that would take for ever. I will however attach my most recent CV at the end of this chapter for you to peruse and possibly employ me if you like what you see.

I'm sure Chris will enjoy it.

I've made some notes . . .

I'll also quickly tell you about the worst job I've ever had.

When I was with my ex-boyfriend he often mocked me for not having a proper job. I was singing on weekends, earning in one night roughly what people on the minimum wage would earn in a full week.

Seeing as he was Joe Public and knew bot all about the entertainment business, he didn't understand this concept, and seeing as I was naive and stupid at the time I caved and got myself a 'real job'.

Sorry like, but fuck them. If anyone reading this has a talent that they are getting paid for or even just starting to pursue, and you are being told by people close to you to 'give up and get a real job', ignore them, keep going and make sure to give them the finger when you're collecting your BRIT Award.

I was helped along in the process by his mam who worked in a local elderly care home as a receptionist. She assured me she could get me a job and I thought, 'What could be so bad?' I met the manager, got the job, started the following week! Get in! Got myself a PROPER job!

Oh, my word. What a job it was . . .

I have the utmost respect for people who work in care. It is both emotionally and physically draining. I would often find myself stroking an elderly lady's hair, crying my eyes out while she told me I was beautiful and how she would be so proud to have me as a daughter. I later found out from her distraught daughters-in-law that she was in fact a bit of a cow and she had made most of their married lives a living hell, but with the onset of her dementia, her personality completely changed and she became an absolute dream. I'd often go to see her for a cheeky little pick-me-up, plus she had sweets. She was always my favourite by far, even after I found out that those moving words that brought me to tears were in fact a little script she reiterated to every female she came across.

I can just see you sitting on the end of her bed, crying, shoving Murray Mints into your gob and saying, 'Tell me again how pretty I am and what a good daughter I'd be, Moira.'

On other shifts, I would often find myself running round the local streets searching for the care home's very own Harry Houdini, AKA George.

George was an elderly gentleman who ran away almost daily.

He was cracking on 85 but I swear to you he could outrun my 25-year-old legs most days! It sometimes took three of us to catch him. One day we had to call the police as we couldn't find him anywhere. The police arrived and we kept on searching. We later found him sitting in someone's garden having a little rest on their garden chairs – he'd hopped the bloody fence! It was at least four foot high! The guy was a medical marvel. We'd spotted him from the back lane and he looked so peaceful that we left him for an extra ten minutes of sun-bathing before we headed back.

The next day they installed an alarm system at the care home to stop him from running away, although I have to admit that I did enjoy the little skive I had while searching for him. The home later got him his own cheeky little sun lounger for the back garden – turns out he just wanted a little kip in the sun. Can't blame him, to be honest.

One perk of my days in care was that while on shift I would get a free meal. I don't think we were supposed to, but we would always steal a bit of whatever was on offer. I've always been a fan of canteen-style dining, and although the chef was pretty disgusting and I'd seen his arse crack more times than I'd seen my own, he did make a really delicious chicken pie.

If you're currently reading this and thinking, 'Rosie, that's nothing! I have an awful job that I hate. I drive to work every day and I dream of my car being involved in an accident with a bus resulting in no injuries for anyone else but a case of minor whiplash and a month on the sick for trauma for me. Maybe a substantial payout from said whiplash a little later down the line. Could get that extension I've been talking about . . .'

I hear you! I really do. I've often thought up the exact same situation in my head while sitting in rush-hour traffic on the Tyne Bridge. To make us all feel better, I took it on myself to find someone with a worse job than anyone I know. I think I may have just found her . . .

Hi Chris and Rosie,

I've been a doctor in Obstetrics and Gynaecology for about eight years now and I have seen many, many things that would amuse the SMA audience greatly.

To date the strangest thing I've ever done was pull a McDonald's cheeseburger from a vagina. In its wrapper. With no gherkin or

relish. They'd waited for a plain
cheeseburger.

Jo

Thank you, Jo. You win.

I have some questions . . .

- Double or single cheeseburger?
- Was it still whole? Like, had they had a bite first?
- Why?
- Had they done it with gherkin or relish in the past and found it to be better plain?
- Was it still warm?
- Are we being sponsored by McDonald's or is Rosie hungry because we've mentioned them fucking loads?!

Thank you for your time.

Although my darling wife has indeed had more jobs than me, I've still had a good few now that I'm looking back. I'll not be putting my CV on here as I've not got one any more since I've been a professional comedian for over a decade . . . although sometimes I feel like I should have one as I have many, MANY anxiety dreams where comedy is just 'over' for some reason and I have to either go back to uni or go and get a normal job. In the dream I'm always saying, 'But I'm a comedian, I've been on TV and everything', and the person interviewing me is replying,

'So you've been unemployed for ten years?' I wake up in a cold sweat.

My first job was doing a paper round when I was about 12. I used to do just the evening paper on my parents' estate and the estate next to it. It was pretty easy and I actually really enjoyed it. I still remember how BUZZING I was when I got my first paper bag. I literally rode my bike to my auntie's house to show my cousin! They lived on one of the estates. They weren't on my route because they got their paper from a different shop (JUDAS) but the person next door was, and they got a paper called *The World's Fair* or something . . . I genuinely think it was about fair-grounds. I remember I planned my entrance and big reveal of my paper bag (and paper round) by walking into my auntie's house with my bag on my shoulder and shouting, 'YOUR NEIGHBOURS GET A WEIRD PAPER!' God, I thought I was brilliant.

I can see you doing this. It makes me want to vomit.

My paper round saga was a little bit like a movie about drug dealers, like *Blow* or *Scarface*. It started out brilliantly, but in the end it all went to shit . . . because I got greedy.

I'm sorry like, Chris, but you can't be comparing your paper round of two posh cul-de-sacs in South Shields to drug lord Tony Montana in *Scarface*.

I started off doing just evenings. No worries at all. Two estates right next to each other. Easy. I then took on the Sunday morning leg of the paper round. Good God, that bag was heavy! It was absolute agony carrying those fuckers. I remember the first time I got on my bike with the bag over my shoulder I literally toppled into a hedge.

I also used to accidentally shred the papers up as I was trying to get them into the skinny little letterboxes on everyone's shitty UPVC doors. I would regularly have to stick the outside ten or so pages that had come off in the struggle through the letterbox afterwards like ripped-up wrapping paper. It's literally just occurred to me now that I should have either rung on the doorbell or taken the papers apart . . . literally just now, twenty years later.

THEN I decided that I wanted more of that sweet, sweet moolah, and I took on a weekday morning paper round . . . except the estates didn't have a weekday morning round – this round was in the streets near my school that I was only slightly familiar with.

That wouldn't have stopped Tony Montana . . .

It. Was. Hell.

I had to be up at 5 a.m. and I was devastated about it. Winter was rolling in so I was getting frostbite in my face while speeding up and down the streets on my BMX trying to find roads I'd never heard of. On one occasion I rode home crying my eyes out at about 7 a.m. because I couldn't find 'Ede Avenue' (I still remember the name of it). This was before mobile phones or GPS or anything so I had to go home and ask my dad. He was on the drive busy packing his van for work but he saw the state I was in – half a bag of undelivered papers, tears of frustration frozen solid to my cheeks. So he jumped on my bike and I jumped on the stunt pegs on the back with my paper bag and we sped off and found the street. He did the rest of the round with me too.

I quit that night.

What a legend my dad is though. And what the fuck must anyone who saw us that morning have thought?

After that I was out of the working world until I got a job at All:Sports on King Street in South Shields. This was my first proper job and I only got £2.75 an hour for it. I always thought this was shitty pay . . . but didn't realize just how shit until Rosie said she was on £2.50 when she was only 14.

So after tax, 16-year-old me was getting less than 14-year-old Rosie (and she was getting free sweets!). Absolute disgrace.

Sucker!

I was only on a four-hour-a-week contract so I only came out with about £40 a month from All:Sports. It was a pointless job. I quit it when I got a job at trendy (at the time) clothes shop USC . . . but I accidentally showed up at the induction a month early. In my panic that I'd be skint for a month (fuck knows what I was thinking, I was only down £40!!), I got a mate of mine to get me a job at the Stadium of Light as a waiter.

The Stadium of Light Conference and Banqueting Department was essentially a youth club that you got paid to go to. All of the staff were either at sixth form, college or uni. We all went out together on any nights off we managed to get, and I made some really good mates while I was there. Despite the fact that

I don't give a toss about football, it was easily one of the best REAL jobs I've ever had.

(I say REAL because there is not one moment that goes by where I can't believe my luck that I get to stand on stage and piss about for a living. Although, writing a book and doing a podcast with my wife feels A LOT MORE LIKE ACTUAL WORK.)

At the stadium I was a Silver Service waiter. Meaning, it was all pretty posh in the main banqueting suite and I would go around the tables in a prim and proper fashion, serving each guest their meat from a giant silver platter on my left arm using a fork and spoon in my right hand like a pair of tongs . . . it's a tricky skill to master and I can still do it to this day. Why the fuck we didn't just use tongs was beyond me, but apparently, this was posher. We also had to do a thing called 'crumbing down' which to this day is the most degrading thing I have ever done . . . and I have told entire theatres of people about the time I had worms.

True story.

Crumbing down is where you walk around the table in-between courses and, using a napkin that has been folded into a little hand-sized triangle, sweep the crumbs from in front of the customer on to a little plate in your other hand. I had to do it to a table of Sunderland Youth Team players once. It was awful. They were a table of ten cocky little wankers. All about 15 years old, with overly gelled hair, stinking of CK One and Deep Heat. They found it absolutely hilarious that this 19-year-old lad was having to sweep crumbs up for them and they kept ripping bread up to add more. My face was a shade of red that I don't think it's ever reached again since. I hope they have all subsequently been dropped from the team or been badly injured and their dreams are shattered and they can never kick a fucking ball again.

Bit intense.

I remember being told off in the kitchen that night for shouting something very similar to this to all the other staff as I stood over the bin eating pigs in blankets from the silver platter.

I was wondering if you nicked the food! Fantastic behaviour.

I used to do that a lot. When it was a Christmas dinner function I would be serving the turkey with pigs in blankets, and if a customer didn't want their allocated little sausage wrapped in bacon (WHY?! It's the best bit! Fucking idiots), I would take them back to the kitchen on the tray and eat them over the bin . . . Once someone just wanted veg and no turkey or sausage. A customer next to them said, 'Can I have it then?' and I claimed it was against the rules. He was livid and complained about me to my team leader, but by this time I was back in the kitchen eating that turkey breast with my hands over a bin . . . so who's really the winner here?

Not you, Chris. Sorry, babe, but eating turkey over a bin is not winning. Also, I think that person may have been a vegetarian. Just throwing that out there.

I always try to tip waiters who do a good job now as I remember what it was like to get that extra cash injection on a gruelling night of service. The greatest tip I ever got was £60, from one guy! It might not have been the biggest tip I ever got, but it was the greatest in the way that it happened. I mean, technically it wasn't a tip and I did actually (TECHNICALLY) steal from the company to get it, but just hear me out . . .

It was a Saturday-night wedding party in one of the less formal rooms in the stadium and I was working behind the bar. I'd been working the match all day on Box Level and my box was Number 52, right at the end of the corridor next to the Sky Broadcasting suite. Now when I say 'corridor' I mean the longest corridor you have ever seen. It literally stretched three quarters of the way around the entire stadium, like the Large Hadron Collider built by CERN. So I would always have to get there about an hour before I actually started my shift to secure myself one of the lesser spotted and extremely rare trolleys that were as common as unicorn shit in that place. If I didn't get one, I would spend the entire day carrying crates of lager and platters of food bloody miles. I'd been in early and I was exhausted even before my additional bar shift is what I'm getting at here.

I was standing behind the bar dealing with drunken and rude wedding-party guests all night when a man approached looking like he was about to jump over the bar and smash my face in. He just looked furious. He was a bit taller than me, a bit wider than me, a lot older than me. He was clutching a wad of £20 notes in his left hand, wearing a rather disgusting short-sleeved orange and red checkered shirt, and his face was a shade of drunken and angry red that almost led me to believe he may have been in the midst of being bullied by some Sunderland Youth Team players. (The shirt may have made it look redder than it was, to be fair.) He wasn't being bullied by over-gelled 15-year-olds. He was busy having a rather heated argument with a man further down the bar. About what? I didn't know. But he was LIVID.

I bet he was a drug dealer. He sounds just like a drug dealer, that's exactly what they wear.

He stood and demanded two pints of lager, four bottles of WKD Blue (classy) and a double Jack Daniel's and Coke. (I hear you all cry: 'Chris, this was years ago! How do you remember the EXACT order?' – You'll see.)

While reeling off this order to me he was still exchanging angry words with this other guy down the bar to his right. It was basically a collection of random:

'Oh yeah?!'

'Will you, yeah?!'

'Will you fuck?'

'Piss off, mate!'

No real narrative for me to follow. It just kept getting louder and angrier the entire time I was doing the order.

Ooooh, this is exciting! Bet that other bloke owes him drug money.

Now, I had the two pints pulled and on the bar, I had the four bottles of WKD Blue on the bar but as yet unopened, and I was about to do the JD and Coke when the bloke lost his rag. He flung himself at this other guy and the two of them started kicking the shit out of each other . . . He was so fast that I almost wouldn't have realized he'd done it, and he'd have just vanished out of my line of sight . . . if he hadn't quickly THROWN the wad of £20 notes in his hand right into my face first! They hit my face, dropped down and I quickly pinned them against my chest with my hands, concealing them and at the same time adopting a startled pose of 'Oh my gosh, these men are fighting!'

The doormen swiftly removed both guys from the party and I quickly put the bottles back in the fridge, poured the two pints down the sink, and pocketed my £60 tip. Yes, I should have handed the money in, and I should have definitely used it to pay for the two pints that had come out of the barrel and ended up in the sink . . . but I feel I was within my rights to keep the whole £60, if only for the trauma of what I had witnessed that evening with my own two eyes . . . It really was a disgusting shirt.

I can't believe I'm married to a thief! And drug money too! This is shameful, Chris, utterly shameful. You are Tony Montana. Tony Montana of the North East!

I left the stadium about a year later for a better-paid job (greedy again) at the Inland Revenue.

'YOU WANNA FUCK WITH ME?!?' – Tony Montana/ Chris Ramsey.

I still have no idea to this day what I was doing there. I could tell you what I was doing in the sense of literally talk you through the stuff I did, but I have no idea what it was for. It was something to do with letting people know they either had or hadn't made some kind of payment. Honestly, every time I get a letter from the Inland Revenue I take it with a pinch of salt because it's probably being sent out by a useless prick like me.

This concerns me.

This Inland Revenue job was a temporary contract and when it ended we all went out on a staff night out. I got far too drunk on social club price Jack Daniel's and Coke, was sick in the taxi on the way home and had to get my job back at the stadium the very next day to pay my mam and dad back the £60 fine from the taxi driver.

I worked at the stadium again until I started uni and got my student loan . . .

When that ran out I had to get a job in the New Crown Pub in South Shields, and at the same time, I started stand-up comedy. I remember phoning up and begging for a shift swap as I had a spot at the Hyena Comedy Cafe in Newcastle one night. Comedy took off and I quit working in the pub a little while later.

People always ask how I got into comedy. If it was something I always wanted to do. If it was something I always thought I could do. And the answer is weird . . . It wasn't until I did it that I knew it was something I'd always wanted to do. Basically, I had no idea stand-up comedy was a thing until I started doing it. I had stand-up videos and I had seen stand-up on TV, but I always thought that they were just famous people who had decided to do a show in front of an audience one night for the hell of it. I always thought they did something else to get famous and fill the theatre. I had seen Jim Davidson hosting *Big Break* and just assumed he was a TV host first. I had seen Lee Evans in *There's Something About Mary* and *Mouse Hunt* so just assumed he was a film star first. Then Ricky Gervais weirdly cemented this belief for me by becoming famous for creating *The Office* then quite literally saying, 'I'm going to have a pop at stand-up.'

I had no idea there was an established route from being a normal guy and being on TV as a comedian that was a path I could actually follow, until my mate Carl Hutchinson told me one day he was going to an open mic night. Listeners to the podcast will be overjoyed that Carl has turned up in the book, and I'm sure Rosie will have something to say.

I've been waiting for him to pop up.

I can still remember the genuine excitement and panic I felt when he explained to me that you could just go to a venue and get up on stage and tell some stories and jokes . . . and that he was going to do it! The best way I can describe the feeling: it was like I was out looking around the shops for something in particular that I couldn't find, then I bumped into Carl and he told me there was ONE LEFT in the shop around the corner but I had to quickly go and get it. That was the feeling. Panic and excitement and impatience to get up and have a go myself.

I got in contact with the guy who ran the gig, Al Dawes. Long Live Comedy took place on a Tuesday night above the Dog and Parrot pub in Newcastle, and Al told me I could get on in a month to do a spot. I went to Asda the next day and bought a navy blue hardback notebook and a pen and began to write down everything I could think of. Luckily I had to go for an STI check during that month too . . . so the material just wrote itself!

Rank.

After my first five-minute set (which went remarkably well considering I was telling a room full of strangers about getting a rod shoved down the end of my dick) I was telling people I was a comedian. Honestly, I was no longer a student, I was a comedian. I told everyone. And that was that.

And when comedy goes tits up, I'll obviously go back to the stadium again.

They'll not have you back after this, Chris – remember that £60? 'Every day above ground is a good day.' – Tony Montana/ Chris Ramsey.

The Illustrious Career of Rosie Ramsey

Profile

A dedicated, hard-working, focused and successful individual who displays energy and enthusiasm in every aspect of work. A strong team player, with exceptional motivational skills, which have contributed to providing a sound platform for success. Extremely results-orientated and always looking to improve to ensure that all objectives and expectations are reached/exceeded.

Right, whose CV have you copied this off?!

Kate (my sister). Also, just to clarify, this is an old CV. This is before my Instagram page took off and I became an author and one of the UK's top podcasters. #justsaying

As a potential employer I would read this sentence of your CV, find it arrogant and you would not get the job. #justsaying

Qualifications

NCFE Level 2 Qualified Teaching Assistant

1997–2002 St Wilfrid's RC Comprehensive School, Harton Lane, South Shields
  8 GCSEs, including English Lit. & Lang., Drama, Maths & Science

I got 12 . . .

Good for you.

Work History (1998–2017)

July 2015–present. **Full-time parent.** *I decided to leave my last position as I wanted to be a full-time mother. Now that my little boy is two years old I feel ready to return to work.*

Lazy.

February 2014–July 2015 (four months' maternity leave included). Capital FM/Global – **DriveTime radio presenter.** *While working as a teaching assistant I volunteered at a student radio station. During this time I was given the early-morning breakfast show which I would do before work three mornings a week. After a year of volunteering I was asked to work for Capital FM North East which saw me there for a year. I would deliver the afternoon show five days a week and work with my co-host daily to create features and maintain all our social media pages.*

Smashed it, to be fair.

January 2011–February 2014. Agency work – **Teaching Assistant.**
*I gained my Level 2 Teaching Assistant qualification by attending
a night-time course. My role required me to assist the class teacher
with everyday classroom tasks. This was work through an agency
so I worked in many schools.*

Ah yes, I remember fondly the days where Rosie would catch
EVERY SINGLE germ, sniffle, cold and flu from the kids and
bring them into our house. What a time!

April 2010–January 2011. Dorothy Perkins – **Sales Assistant.**
*Working in a busy town centre store, assisting customers with
their purchases, full till responsibilities, handling cash, dealing
with customer complaints and refunds. Maintaining all standards
of the store.*

Full till responsibilities?! Handling cash?! You might as well have
written 'I'm not a thief'.

March 2010–April 2010. **Lead Female Vocalist.** *Touring the
north of England in a five-piece cabaret show band, weekend
work only.*

Get a real job!

June 2010–October 2010. Southern Cross Residential Home –
Care Assistant. *Working as a care assistant in a busy care home,
this was a temporary contract.*

Duties included:

Devouring sweets and compliments from vulnerable old ladies

Being outrun by old men

Looking at the chef's arse crack

Eating chicken pie

October 2009–March 2010. Average Joe Productions – **Lead Female Vocalist.** *Touring the country in a five-piece cabaret show band.*

Get a real fucking job!

March–October 2009. The Production Associates, Thomson Gold, Rhodes – **Production Cast.** *Return contract.*

December 2008–March 2009. Bar Palma, Ocean Road, South Shields, Tyne and Wear – **Bar Person.** *This was a part-time position, meaning I worked weekends only. My duties in this role were serving drinks, handling cash and cleaning the bar area.*

Genuinely remember when you worked here and I used to try and give you the eye . . . with no success.

March–November 2008. The Production Associates, Thomson Gold, Rhodes – **Production Cast.** *Singer/dancer for production team based in Rhodes. This was an eight-month summer contract due to start again in April 2009.*

'I lived in Rhodes'; 'I used to work in Rhodes, Chris'; 'We should go to Rhodes, Chris'; 'Have you ever been to Rhodes, Chris? I used to work there'; 'We should stay at the hotel I used to work in, in Rhodes'; 'I know a little bit of Greek!'; 'Do you like tzatziki?'

October 2007–February 2008. River Island, Waterloo Square, South Shields, Tyne and Wear – **Christmas Temp Sales Assistant**. *Working in this very busy town centre store as part of the sales team. My main duties included: serving and advising customers, full till responsibilities, i.e. exchanges and refunds, handling cash, achieving set sales targets.*

'I would later be promoted to Dorothy Perkins down the road . . . I'm not a thief.'

March 2007–March 2008. Cabaret Show Band – **Lead Vocalist**. *One-year position touring in a five-piece cabaret band.*

FOR FUCK'S SAKE, GET A REAL JOB!!

2006–2007. RLS Employment, Bridge House, Sunderland, Tyne and Wear – **Recruitment Consultant**. *I started off with this company as a receptionist, then later received a promotion to the recruitment side of the business. I would interview candidates, select workers for jobs, organize transport to and from jobs and also organize all accommodation for overnight stays.*

Bit annoying, as you haven't booked a train ticket yourself since we got together.

2006 – RLS Employment, Bridge House, Sunderland, Tyne and Wear – **Receptionist**. *My duties included taking calls, arranging meetings, making teas and coffees for staff members and clients, organizing diaries, typing company letters.*

'Rosie, you're taking these calls like a legend, my diary is immaculate, the letters have never been better and this tea is DELICIOUS! You're a recruitment consultant now!'

2006 – NEW (North East Workforce), Collingwood Street, Newcastle upon Tyne – **Admin Work**. *I joined this agency and received a large amount of temporary work, sometimes different positions every other day, which meant travelling to different destinations. This work was usually receptionist or office based in general. I enjoyed this very much as I love meeting new people and it was great being able to help out when office staff were in need.*

'It was great being able to help out when office staff were in need' – translation: I was skint and didn't have a gig that day.

2005 – The Customs House, Dick Whittington – **Principal Girl**. *I was offered the position of principal girl at my local theatre in South Shields after auditioning earlier that year. This was my first major role and I thoroughly enjoyed it. I followed on to do the next year also, which was* Aladdin.

2005 – United Carlton, Team Valley Trading Estate, Gateshead – **Meter Reader.** *I got this job through an agency called All Temps based in South Shields. My duties included calling companies with one of our photocopying machines and taking the meter reading, also asking how the machine was running and so on. I was later promoted to receptionist for the same company in the main office. My main tasks were to answer and direct calls on the twelve-line phone, organize meetings with clients, meet and greet clients at the main door, direct post, type letters and other admin tasks.*

I've literally never been promoted in any job I've ever had and I'm a bit jealous.

2005 – Pontins Brean Sands, Somerset – **Blue Coat.** *This was my first professional performance-based role at the age of 18. I performed in evening shows as lead vocalist and I also compered during the day and socialized with guests of all ages.*

I've seen the videos of this and I'd like to take issue with the phrase 'professional performance'.

2004 – Inland Revenue, Hebburn – **Data Entry** *(four-month contract). During my time in this role I learnt how to touch-type, which I found extremely useful and use to this day. My main duties were to enter tax return data into a computer system.*

See . . . no one knew what the fuck they were doing there.

*2004 – The Body Shop, Sunderland Bridges – **Sales Assistant**. This store is based in a very busy shopping centre so I managed to use my new-found selling skills to their full advantage. I greeted customers, advised them on products, demonstrated products and also handled cash and dealt with returns and complaints.*

'I didn't steal any soap.'

*2003 – The Gadget Shop, Eldon Square – **Sales Assistant**. I started this job while at college and liked it so much that I left college and took on a full-time contract as I felt college was not benefiting me at that particular time in my life and I'd rather be out earning some money and learning some much-needed life skills. I took to my new role very well and was given a lot of responsibility even though I was the tender age of 16. I handled cash and dealt with complaints and returns. I advised customers on new and existing gadgets in the store, and it was my first real taste of working as part of a team.*

I know you got to stand at the front of the store playing with remote control helicopters and I'm very jealous. Bit weird writing 'tender age of 16' on a CV though . . . just a bit creepy.

*1998–2002 – Local Ice Cream Parlour, South Shields – **Waitress**. I was 14 years old and still at school when I started this job. I worked all day Saturday and Sunday and also one early evening during the week. My main duties included serving customers food and drink in the busy café and serving at the ice cream counter situated at the front of the café. I most importantly gained* *experience in customer service which I have found beneficial in every job I have had since.*

Interests

I am a very active and energetic person who enjoys various activities to promote personal fitness.

BOLLOCKS!

I enjoy socializing and meeting new people, and spending time with my family and friends is extremely important to me.

'I drink at the weekend, snog strangers on a Saturday night, then go to my mam's house for a hung-over Sunday dinner.'

As you can see from my CV, singing and performing have always been a passion of mine and performance has at times been my main job. I feel that the confidence I have gained through my years of experience in this field helps me a lot in aspects of other jobs, including delivering great customer service, which I also expect to be delivered to myself.

'I want to be famous, but I'll happily come and work in your shithole company until that happens.'

Basically, yes.

Dark Days

There's light at the end of the tunnel . . .

If you're reading this now and you're currently happily (or unhappily) married, I'm going to take you back.

Back to your single days . . .

Not the good ones when you're a young, hot, fresh-blooded teen, without a care in the world, necking on with randomers in a club for sport. Never getting a hangover and being able to party till 2 a.m. and still get up and go to work at 8 a.m.

No.

I'm taking you back to the dark days.

The in-between relationship days.

The drink yourself silly every weekend, sleep with strangers just so you don't have to be alone another night, crying into your cheesy chips and garlic sauce on Christmas Eve days.

If you've never experienced these days then I envy you, I really do.

I've been there myself.

Being single on the wrong side of 25 wondering if you'll ever meet someone? Why is everyone an utter chode? Why didn't I just stay with my ex? At least I'd not be crying into my cheesy garlic chips on Christmas Eve. That's a true story, by the way. It takes place on Christmas Eve 2011 and features myself, my best friend Steph, some cheesy garlic chips and my mam.

Picture the scene . . .

It's 12:30 a.m. Steph and I have been out on the drink since 5 p.m. We are both single AF.

After a lovely night of dancing to Mariah Carey, drinking and merriment it's time to go home. Steph comes to mine because she is also single, it's Christmas Eve and other than her lonely double bed at her ma and da's house she doesn't have anywhere to be.

We decide to make the most of it and enjoy our cheesy garlic chips together. Problem is we are single AF, probably due on and it's Christmas Eve . . . There was no enjoyment to be had here this night.

I'm hearing all of this sadness, but all I can think of is that I REALLY want some cheesy chips and garlic sauce right now . . .

A lot of crying ensues. Now, when I say a lot, I mean a lot. Back then I could cry for fun . . . but it wasn't fun, I was genuinely absolutely miserable.

I'd recently split up from a long-term relationship. Actually, is three years long-term? I suppose it is when you're 23, isn't it? Anyway, we had very recently split up. We had lived together too so it was made even harder. He moved out of our flat and my mam moved in. It was actually her flat that she had rented to us. I think she was secretly over the moon about us breaking up. Her next plan of action was to get me shacked up again and out of her flat so she could have it all to herself! I see you, Sandra, you little sneaky minx! Aye, I see you.

It's a scary time, being newly single. Especially for a woman, I think.

If you are anything like I was, you want to be married and settled with children before you're 30. But then you'd also like to be with the person you end up marrying for at least three years before anyone starts getting down on one knee. You're probably imagining an engagement of a year too.

Ah balls. I was already three years behind my life plan.

Then let's not forget about the biological clock, ladies. Oh yes! That tick-tock-tocking that once you reach the wrong side of 25 you can hear in the back of your brain like an endless metronome. It's pretty quiet at first but it's definitely there. Tick tock, tick tock.

I never really paid much attention to my biological clock, to be honest. It wasn't until I heard someone mention it on television (I think it was probably on *Real Housewives*?). Apparently once you reach 30 years old your chances of getting pregnant drop to 20 per cent.

Yep, you heard me: TWENTY PER CENT! Well, hang me out to dry. YOU HAVE GOT TO BE KIDDING ME?!?! That is so much pressure!

Imagine getting your medical knowledge from *Real Housewives of Shoutsville County*. Do you see what I'm dealing with here, people?

Why don't men have sperm that ticks? Yes, it too has a shelf life but it's a heck of a lot longer than a woman's. Imagine our eggs are like little green bananas, tough and hard one year, then BOOM, brown and battered the next. While a man's sperm are like a tin of beans, safe and secure for years. You know that you can rely on them, you'll find them at the back of your cupboard. Out of date, yes, but probably perfectly edible. Bit like actual sperm in that respect, really.

Question is, why are we burdened with this immense responsibility to find a mate, settle down, make sure he's not horrific and get impregnated? Honestly, it makes me sick to my stomach. Just like sperm.

I always knew that I wanted a family. It was such a strong feeling that I couldn't ignore it.

I felt like one of those lizards in the nature programmes, that just sits on top of a rock waiting for someone decent to come along and mate with me. Changing my outfits every night out in order to attract someone new. Maybe, if I was lucky, a male lizard would have a fight with another dominant male who was checking me out from afar. The winner takes all. Ah, that would have been pretty nice, made me feel a bit wanted.

I'm sad to admit that this never happened. No men have ever fought over me to win my affection. It would appear that I'm not actually as much of a catch as my mam bigs me up to be. She's been lying to me for YEARS! 'You're beautiful, Rosie! Any boy would be lucky to have you!' Ah really, Sandra? Well, where are they now, eh? Where the hell are they now when I need them? Nowhere to be bastard seen, that's where they are!

Anyway, back to Christmas Eve . . .

I was living with Sandra at the time, in the flat that she owns which my boyfriend had just recently moved out of. The very same flat in which I'd spent the last three Christmases with him.

Steph and I were getting a little carried away with our emotions and we were crying rather loudly, so loud in fact, we woke my mam up. In my defence, it was/is a rather small flat and the walls aren't that thick, so it was inevitable, to be fair.

My mam was understandably a little frustrated as it was indeed Christmas Eve, it was very late and she was definitely not as intoxicated as me and Steph.

We didn't stop crying.

We ended up having an argument because I kissed a boy who I'd complained about to Steph earlier that day. She called me desperate. I got mad. It got really heated. I dropped my cheesy garlic chips on the living-room floor in front of the tree.

This is the real tragedy here.

Sandra lost her temper, told us both to pack it in, sent Steph home and put me to bed.

Santa came. I did not.

The End.

Thankfully Steph and I are still best friends now. She was absolutely bang on about that boy. He was rotten.

Unfortunately, these dark days didn't end that Christmas. Just like a bad smell, they managed to hang on with me all the way through until the next one.

Christmas 2012 was a little different, though. December 2012 is the very month my luck started to change. I finally learnt from all my awful decisions. I took a chance on a boy from my past. Someone who I'd always known but never had a romantic connection with. The boy I used to say hello to in the college corridors, the one with all the hair, the skinny jeans and tight leather jacket.

This boy made me laugh, like really made me laugh. He was kind and thoughtful. He made me feel good about myself and he cared about me from the off. He wanted to be with me and when he would come to my house he'd bring me bars of Dairy Milk.

We enjoyed the same films, we liked the same food. He was my age too! We were both born in the same month! I knew straight away that this was the boy I was going to spend the rest of my life with.

And for the first time in my life, this boy never once questioned my job because, just like me, he didn't have a real job either.

Is this me? This is me, isn't it? Knew them chocolate bars would work.

Ah, the tale of the Festive Garlic-and-Cheese-fuelled Emotional Breakdown. I am very familiar with this little tale. I've heard it multiple times and I'm always blown away by just how sad you'd have to be to actually cry while eating cheesy chips and garlic sauce. I honestly don't think I could even force half a tear out while slopping a load of that into my face. If anything, they would be tears of joy.

The whole 'I need to be settled with kids by the time I'm 30' thing never entered my head when I was single. Like, never. I actually didn't even know that I wanted a family until Rosie told me I did . . .

Wow. Don't remember holding a gun to your head, Chris.

Then that was that. I can totally get on board with the loneliness thing though.

Just to let you know, sperm lasts for years. As long as you have a good egg, men can implant well into their sixties.

At the risk of ruining my manly reputation here (almost couldn't type that for laughing), I used to get proper lonely when I was single. You miss cuddles, you miss having someone to share stuff with, and I really missed having someone to phone in the night, like on the way back from gigs. Annoyingly when I ring Rosie now she's normally too busy watching TV to chat and says she'll just see me when I get in . . . She probably needs to concentrate fully on all that high-level scientific knowledge being taught by the *Real Housewives* . . .

You're absolutely right. Proper highbrow stuff is the *RH*.

Do It Yawn-Self

I recently met my cousin for lunch when she immediately started complaining that she was extremely tired. She told me that her husband had kept her awake all night tossing and turning. Apparently, to resolve this, he got up to go to the toilet and when he came back fell straight to sleep. In my head I assumed that maybe he had a funny tummy, or was feeling a bit sick, but how wrong I was. She then calmly and casually said, 'Obviously he went to the toilet to wank.' Clearly my face displayed a confused look as she then explained that her husband's method of solving insomnia is to have some 'alone time'.

My first question: is this normal? As I understand, wanking does make boys sleepy, but is it normal for this to be your main method of getting to sleep? Why not put on a podcast, count sheep – you know, normal ways?

However, the conversation did not end there. While trying to comprehend if this was normal, but outwardly nodding along so she

didn't think I was a prude, she proceeded to
tell me that she's completely fine with it
now that he leaves the bedroom to sort
himself out . . . Apparently, in the past she
had woken up to the bed shaking and turned
to see her boyfriend, dick in hand, trying
to make himself 'sleepy' (on multiple
occasions!). Because she explained the story
so casually and also quite loudly for other
diners to hear, I've wondered if maybe this
is more common than I thought.

So my second question: Rosie, how would you
feel if you woke up to Chris doing this?

Martha

Quite frankly, babe, I'd be mortified.

Like you, I don't see myself as a prude. Take this book, for
example – it's pretty honest, right? I love it, I thrive on it. But
this, this is on another level.

I am fully aware of the fact that my husband masturbates,
it's totally normal. It'd be a bit weird if he didn't. I would however absolutely not be OK with him doing it in OUR bed
when I am in it. Gross.

Understandably when you live with someone you lose a bit
of your independent identity. It's hard to live the life you had
before. But there must be times when a couple isn't together
and a guy can have a wank when their partner is out. It's honestly as simple as that. I don't think I would be able to have sex

with Chris ever again if every night I heard him 'whacking one off' (sorry, Mam) less than a foot away from me.

What did your cousin do while this was going on? Could her husband hold a conversation at the same time? Surely it takes a modi**cum** (sorry) of concentration to masturbate successfully? How big is their bed? We have a Super King and it's a canny size but I'd still be raging.

All this says to me is that her partner has unfortunately got himself into a terrible routine of having to wank in order to get himself off to sleep. Which I find utterly ridiculous, to be honest. All I can see is him as a manky teenager lying in his bed every night having about ten wanks in-between playing *Call of Duty*, wiping his you-know-what all over his dark red curtains (sorry but he blates had a red room like), leaving all his dirty cups along the window sill so his poor mother has to come and collect them and wash them when her friends come round for coffee, choking on his wank fumes.

Eurgh.

You are not alone in your shock, I'm right there with you, babe. This can't continue, surely? Is there nothing sacred left any more? I suggest that your cousin puts her foot down. It's not a big ask to suggest he stop masturbating to get to sleep. Eeeh, what a selfish little wanker he is (literally).

I've googled it and apparently it doesn't help you get to sleep but it does relax you. How about he tries to meditate? Have a bath before bed?

Recently Robin has been struggling to get to sleep by himself. I've introduced a sticker chart – if he can go to sleep by himself he gets a sticker; once he's filled a row of five stickers he gets a prize of his choosing. Maybe your cousin could intro-duce this too? I mean, she absolutely shouldn't have to as it's ludicrous behaviour, but it's all I can think to suggest other than chopping his willy off.

If Chris was doing this every night I'd hit the bloody roof! I'd leave him. No, sorry, scrap that, I wouldn't leave him, I'd chuck him out. I'd chuck him out and I'd create a fake email account and I'd send an email to every single person he ever happened to meet in the future. The email would read some-thing like this:

```
A word of warning.

He has to masturbate to get to sleep.

Every. Single. Night.

It's not a medical condition, it's just a habit.
```

He'd be furious, I know, but it would serve him bloody right because I'd be scarred for life. I'd have to fork out for therapy because of all the late-night rocking shenanigans I'd had to endure. I'd never be able to trust another man again, living in fear that anyone I welcomed into my bed might have to knock one off in order to kip. Horrific behaviour.

Dear ENTIRE PORN INDUSTRY,

I am sending you this letter (and the above chapter of my book . . . I'm an author) as the main piece of evidence that I believe blows a gigantic hole in one of your most widely used narratives. I, and I'm sure every other man reading this book, feel hurt, betrayed, misled and quite frankly, absolutely furious about this affair.

You have LONG portrayed that a man masturbating is an extremely attractive thing for a woman to see. You have in every single instance portrayed the discovering of the culprit to be a huge aphrodisiac for the lady in question, and in 100 per cent of cases, full sex with said lady has happened as a DIRECT RESULT of the initial wank.

I submit to you the above email and subsequent chapter from a loyal podcast and book fan and my – quite clearly – utterly disgusted wife. It seems pretty obvious to me that you have been lying to men all over the world from day one, and if we are caught masturbating by any member of the opposite sex the last thing we will ever hear is the phrase 'Need some help with that?', 'Mind if I join in?', or the admittedly hilarious but still viciously misleading 'Looks like you need a hand?' Quite the opposite, in fact.

We will, it seems, end up an object of ridicule and shame, and possibly be so upset that we can't even finish the task at hand. As you can see, the very mention of this happening has led my wife to threaten eviction of myself from the family home and even divorce.

I demand that you remove every video using this narrative from the internet before any more men fall victim to this situation. Or at the very least add a warning before the action that clearly outlines the complete fabrication of the entire situation.

Yours, furiously

Chris Ramsey

PS. I suppose next you'll be telling me that the brothers, sisters and stepmothers in your videos aren't actually related?!

Threesomes

Back in university I ended up having a threesome with identical twin guys. I pulled one of them in a bar and kept going back throughout the night. In my drunken state I didn't realize I was actually going to a different person each time - I mean, they looked the same and had similar clothes on. Later on into the night after more drinks were consumed I saw them both stood together and was very confused - long story short they both ended up walking me home and one thing led to another.

This is something quite rare, so I think it's a good story to tell people. I've been chatting to someone on Tinder for quite a while (we've just arranged a date) and the conversation moved to two truths and one lie. Obviously, I included the threesome, because who's actually done that? He guessed incorrectly and I told him it was actually the truth. With that he said he wouldn't ever marry someone that's had

a threesome and decided to reconsider the
date.

So my question is: if either of you had had
a threesome pre getting serious, would you
think differently?

Ashleigh

Firstly, congratulations for managing to find the only non-sleazebag on Tinder! That is quite an achievement! Also, my commiserations that it hasn't worked out – it's always shite when that happens.

Plenty more fish in the sea . . . especially when you catch them two at a time.

Just for clarification to our readers, 'two truths and one lie' is an ice-breaking game which has made its way on to dating sites.

Here's what Google said – this will be easier than me explaining it . . .

> *Two Truths and a Lie is a classic ice-breaker game in which one attempts to identify which of three statements is bogus. Instructions: Have everyone sit in a circle. Each person prepares three statements, two of which are true and one of which is a lie.*

This is actually pretty sweet, I think. Probably makes it a lot easier to find out a bit about someone before the inevitable meet-up in person, although in Ashleigh's case it did the complete opposite, so maybe approach this one with caution.

I'm not judging here, but maybe, just MAYBE, in an ice-breaking game of two truths one lie to get to know a STRANGER ... don't make one of the truths your deepest, darkest secret? You know, best to go with something like 'I make my own wine' or 'I'm allergic to shellfish' and not 'I drunkenly and somewhat accidentally had an incest threesome'. Just a thought. Again, not judging. (OK, I'm judging a bit.)

I used to love shit like this, to be honest. I can imagine a team-building day which includes activities like this game would fill most people with dread, but for me it was a chance to be extravagant and let all my former colleagues know that it was not my destiny to become a full-time recruitment consultant but to in fact be a pop star or a public speaker.

Author was never up there on my to-do list ... hmm, strange that.

Just for the sheer lols, here's what I would say!

- I'm 5 foot 1 inch tall.
- I enjoy long walks along the beach with my family.
- When I worked abroad I developed a bit of a drinking problem and was addicted to late-night skinny-dipping sessions in the neighbouring hotel swimming pool.

Care to hazard a guess, Chris?

You're never 5 foot 1. You're 4 foot 9 at best.

I've been on walks with OUR family and rarely are they enjoyable.

Yeah, that's bang on.

You've done two lies and a truth . . .

I don't think I actually understand the game . . . Anyway . . .

No, Ashleigh, unfortunately I've never had a threesome myself, as to be totally honest with you they freak me the F out.

Unfortunately?!

I struggle to give my whole attention to just one person, let alone two people or more at the same time. Plus I can imagine them to get extremely messy and uncomfortable afterwards which would make me want to die inside, so I've always just left them.

I have been asked to partake in a couple of threesomes before, which I declined profusely. Also, I've said 'a couple' just to show off. In fact it was only the one time and I'm not even quite sure they were asking me. I'm still quietly confident that I would be threesome material, but it's not my cup of tea.

I do however absolutely NOT judge anyone who has dabbled in these 'somes' situations. As long as all parties are consensual then I say go for it.

It's a shame but I don't personally know anyone who has ever really truly enjoyed a threesome. They've just always been a hazy, haphazard operation that they'd happily bury somewhere deep and forget it ever happened.

A lot of them take place at music festivals while young and intoxicated, carefree living in a field having multiple lovers like some sort of seventies movie. I can imagine the leaving day of the festival, everyone feeling regretful and hoping to God they haven't caught a nasty disease or got pregnant. Awks.

I've never been to a festival before. It's never been at the top of my agenda.

I bloody love live music and outdoor gigs, but I was once told a story of a young girl who fell down the toilet at Leeds festival trying to retrieve her purse when it fell down the bog. She was in there for hours and as there's no showers they had to hose her down. I imagine it was in public and I imagine she had to be sent to hospital.

I couldn't get the image out of my head. It's put me off for life, I swear.

I think they made T-shirts and everything. Poor girl.

I think you'll find her nickname was actually 'poo girl'.

Also, the not being able to get washed for days fills me with dread. I'm not even an overly clean person but not being able to have a shower for three days during the summer is rank. And another thing – apparently daft drunk lads wee and jump on tents. I'd end up getting mad and confronting them, a fight would ensue and I'd get arrested. It's just not worth it in my eyes.

A hundred per cent agree on this (not the fighting bit, I'd just sit in my collapsed, piss-soaked tent and cry my eyes out). A load of my mates went to Leeds festival when I was at uni and one day they drew all over each other with a black sharpie . . . and all the ink came off within an hour because of all the sweat, grease and oil that came out of their pores. I could be sick just thinking about it.

Maybe you're sat reading this now and thinking, 'Oh, I could fancy a threesome one day, you know!'

Absolutely not, but carry on.

That's great, good for you. My advice though would be to either get it discreetly out of your system now or wait until you're older and your marriage is falling apart. Might be better odds of enjoyment then, to be honest, but I'm unsure if that actually works as I don't know anyone who has done that. Mam? Dad? HA! Ew. I hate myself.

Wow, this book is just . . . Well, I have no idea what's happening, to be honest, but I'm going with it. (Praying my Dad never reads it.)

Unfortunately, as I can see from the content of your email, your Tinder contact is not a fan of threesomes, not one bit.

I find it sad that he has judged you so cruelly on this before actually getting to know you. I would suggest not contacting him again as he is clearly extremely opinionated and is looking for the perfect person who probably doesn't exist. I also don't think he's on the correct dating site. I think Match.com or something along those lines would be much more suitable.

I do have some questions of my own for you re the 'twin

threesome' if you don't mind. Not for any other reason than my curiosity is going wild over here.

- What were their names?
- Did they have rhyming names?
- Was it weird saying them out loud? Say were they called Peter and Paul or Ky and Ry? I'm not sure I could have not laughed, to be honest.
- Where did the act take place?
- Did they share a room?
- Did you get the suspicion that they do this often? Because I would bet my house that they do.

I'd bet my life on it.

- Did you prefer one over the other?
- Would you do it again?
- How identical were they exactly? (Did they have matching willies?)

Knew this was what you were getting at ... All of the other questions were just building up to this – you don't give a shit if their names rhymed or not!

Please, if you don't mind emailing in again, genuinely curious over here. Thank you.

For the love of God, no photos.

Now, to the judgemental Tinder bloke.

Here's the thing: when Chris and I first got together I knew pretty soon that he was the one for me, it just clicked. Plus I was 26, I'd had some crap boyfriends and Chris was a good, solid marital choice. I could have done a lot worse, believe me.

I'm literally framing this paragraph for use in arguments.

When we got engaged we decided to tell each other everything about our pasts. Now when I say everything, I mean EVERYTHING. It was an extremely strange conversation to have with the person you love and want to spend the rest of your life with, but we thought it was important that we knew everything about each other before we went into a marriage together. Thankfully neither of us were put off and we often have a little laugh together about our shite life choices and how grown-up we are now.

If you aren't a very trusting person and have been hurt in the past, then I think this is an absolutely vital thing to do in order to have a successful relationship. Failing that, there's always a lie detector test, but unfortunately you'll have to fork out for it yourselves as they've taken Jeremy Kyle off air.

Skeletons in your cupboards are scary both literally and figuratively. I've heard of so many relationships breaking down because of lack of communication, or because one will find something out about the other's past that they've failed to disclose.

I believe honesty is always the best policy. I think the most heart-breaking thing for me would be if I was in a relationship and something came back from my past to bite me in the arse and my partner didn't know and judged me. I would be devastated.

Hence why we told each other everything.

Well I did, at least . . .

Yep, same. I remember the night we did that well: bottle of wine, TV off, reliving harrowing, embarrassing and scary things from the crypts of my love life while at the same time praying that something unfathomably horrific wasn't about to fall out of the mouth of the woman I'd just proposed to . . . GREAT TIMES!

I've said it before and I'll say it again – I have no idea how people have threesomes. From the initiation of one through all of the admin (personal space and fluids) to the moment you have to mop those fluids up – it absolutely baffles me that they are a thing.

I used to find it very hard to initiate sex with the opposite sex when I was single, so all I can think is that it's the same problem, squared. People always say 'it just happened' or 'one thing led to another' when describing how a threesome took place . . . HOW? How did THREE PEOPLE end up just having sex? It must be all about finding like-minded people who are all the same level of secure with themselves, their sexuality and confidence to just LET IT HAPPEN. I know if I was ever in this situation I would literally be shouting out loud, 'GUYS?! ARE WE HAVING A THREESOME?! IS THIS HAPPENING?! WTF?!'

I just don't know how I would conduct myself throughout . . . Who decides whose turn it is? Who decides where you stand/ sit/lie? Who decides where or indeed when you all finish? I'm honestly having a minor panic attack while typing this. I imagine it'll be like moving a sofa into a house with your mate, except you're both naked and the sofa is a lady, and saying, 'Bit higher at your end, Darren mate' would kill the mood.

I had a mate who told me about a threesome he had once, and it put me off the idea even more . . . It was him and his friend (male) and a girl. This is how they tend to happen mostly, isn't it? Am I right? I don't think any bloke has ever had two girls outside of the porn industry. I think it's probably easier to find two male perverts in the same bar than two female.

So, the story goes . . . They are both involved with the girl simultaneously but then his mate goes for a little sit-down on a chair across the room for a moment, to catch his breath apparently (must have been a smoker). While he's sitting there, he's 'keeping himself going', shall we say. At this point, mid-thrusts, my mate turns round to glance at his friend (no idea why you would do this, but anyway) and catches his mate watching the whole thing happening while saying, 'Go on, Phil! Go on, mate!' Now I don't know about you, dear reader, but there is nothing that would put me off the task at hand like an out of breath, masturbating cheerleader sitting on a chair in the same room. NO THANKS.

Mile-High Wanky-Panky

I was on a flight from New York to
Manchester stopping in Dublin, and I was sat
next to an American woman. We got chatting
and I soon realized, 'Oh, she's a bit odd.'
She didn't really understand about personal
space and got really close when speaking
and even went so far as to ask me why I
was taking the pills I was taking. So
I moved over to the window seat and fell
asleep.

I woke up to the man across the aisle with
his cock and balls fully out, playing with
himself. To my horror, I checked in with my
seat mate to see if she was just as
mortified, but she had a tit hanging out,
and her hands under her blanket, and they
were staring at each other! I WAS MORTIFIED,
but I thought, 'They must do this a lot and
that's how they get their kicks.' The man
saw that I was awake but didn't even
flinch - he just carried on while looking
between me and the girl. I closed my eyes

and waited for it to stop. I opened my eyes about ten minutes later, and they were both gone. I assumed they went to the bathroom to finish each other off. I looked over to see who was sat next to the man, and it was two people who were sleeping – a man of about 20 and a woman of about 60. A few minutes later the woman woke up and started looking around. Then Mr Peep Show returned to his seat AND GAVE THE WOMAN WHO WAS PREVIOUSLY SLEEPING A KISS. My seat mate returned but she and the old man whose cock is now burned into my brain didn't speak to each other for the rest of the flight. The wheels touched down in Dublin and now I'm fully invested in what's going on here. So I follow them because I have a three-hour layover. From what I could tell, the man and woman who engaged in their little peep show had never met each other before, and the man, sleeping woman and twentyish-year-old man were a family (Mum, Dad and son).

I spoke to the airline about it and now have an upgrade for my return flight back to NY . . . My question is, what is the best perk you've ever got from making a complaint?

Rosie, a frequent flier

Sorry, WHAT?

I'm horrified by this. You poor innocent lamb! Why in God's name are people so absolutely disgusting? I'm utterly FLABBERGASTED by this. And I cannot believe that they didn't stop once you'd woken up. To be totally honest – and I know I shouldn't laugh because it is absolutely awful – but I did let out a little chuckle at the fact that you had to pretend you were still asleep so that they could finish their 'across the aisle wank'. So rank, man.

I am full to the brim with questions (I can imagine Chris is too).

I AM GOING TO BURST.

First of all, I'm desperate to know how this started. I wonder who instigated it? Him or her? Do you think he is a flasher and tries it all the time just on the off-chance someone will be up for it? She may have started it by 'accidentally' (on purpose) lobbing her boob out and seeing if he was looking thus getting the ball rolling . . . Was it the noise of it all that woke you up? I wonder.

AS IF HE WAS WITH HIS FAMILY?! WHAT A CREEP!!

OMG. Do you think that they are part of some sordid, dark internet site that enables public wankers to chat and plan to meet up? Do you think they planned this trip?! Although that is an awfully expensive trip to make for a bit of mile-high wanky-panky. Oooooh, maybe they're high-flying business people and this is how they relax? I'm jumping to conclusions, I know, but can you imagine seeing this!! I can't believe you didn't say anything!

I'm so glad that you decided to follow them once the plane landed, because if you'd left us hanging I'd be gutted. High five to you, Rosie (great name btw).

Just quickly want to focus on your upgrade for a second. This sounds rather suspicious to me . . . My mind is again jumping to huge conclusions here, but hear me out.

What if the man or woman owns said airline and they do this frequently? The airline didn't have to give you an upgrade. You could have been making it all up as you didn't have any physical evidence. I BET this happens on the regs and they're having to give out upgrades left, right and centre. They must be losing a fortune! All due to those dirty perverts. I'd be livid if I was their accountant.

Anyway, that's what I think happened. I'm sticking with it.

Back to your question . . .

I only started complaining recently, actually. I was brought up with ridiculously good manners – so good, in fact, that I could have been served a lukewarm bowl of piss in a restaurant and my parents would have made me eat it. This inability to complain has been quite crippling over the years, but I'm getting much better at it now.

I complained that our hotel room was right next to the lift a few weeks ago and the hotel switched our room! A few years ago I wouldn't have said a thing and been devastated my whole stay.

Chris was so proud of me. Heck, I was proud of me! Complaining is mint.

OK, I'M SORRY, BUT WHAT THE ACTUAL SHIT IS HAPPENING ON THIS PLANE JOURNEY?!?

I knew you'd like this!

It's time to bust out my catchphrase . . . 'What is wrong with people?!'

The middle paragraph of your email looks like it's been dropped in from some kind of sexual horror film you're writing by accident.

I don't think I've ever read anything that took such a turn so quickly. I genuinely almost fell off my chair when it went:

'So I moved over to the window seat and fell asleep.

[NEW PARAGRAPH]

I woke up to the man across the aisle with his cock and balls fully out . . .'

Cue music – I CAME IN LIKE A WRECKINNNNNNNG BALLLLL!

Jesus.

I'm stunned.

AND THEN for your question to be: 'What is the best perk you've ever had from making a complaint?' – are you on Shuffle? I feel attacked.

Which to be fair is exactly how you must have felt. I mean, first of all, the woman was clearly a strange one what with the personal space thing and asking what pills you were taking, but had you asked me if she would get so bored during your slumber that she would resort to lobbing a tit out for any takers across the aisle, I would have probably gone with no. You learn something new every day. Not that I'm saying she definitely instigated the whole thing; I haven't made my mind up yet.

Honestly, I feel like Netflix need to make a documentary about this.

It would go straight on my list!

Rosie is convinced it's an internet fetish hook-up app or something that brought these perverts together in the air . . . but I think it's more random.

I just think these perverts seem to have an amazing radar to pick someone just like them from a crowd. Then again, I am only taking their successes into consideration here. I imagine that for every:

'I saw him touching his penis across the aisle so I lobbed my tit out and started fingering myself then we went to the bathroom together.'

There are about 100:

'HELP! STEWARDESS, THERE'S A MAN WITH HIS COCK OUT!' horror stories.

Here's a thought . . . Have you ever had a bloke/woman look at you for a bit too long on public transport? Stare at you? Fidget about a bit to catch your attention? What if most of them are attempting to get to the 'show me yours and I'll show you mine' stage, but the moment you don't reciprocate they back down?

Ever thought of that? (Apologies to anyone currently reading this on public transport . . . don't look up.)

I can't believe the bloke was sitting with his family. I literally can't fathom it. I personally can't have a wee at a urinal if there are other people in the public toilet, so the fact that someone has had almost a full wank while surrounded by strangers and sitting next to his sleeping family has left me shocked and appalled. And to come back and give his wife a kiss is just sinister . . .

What would they have done if the air stewards had come round with the drinks?

'Drink, sir?'

'No thanks, I'd like a hot towel though . . . just careful not to put it in my lap.'

The more I think about it, the more I am coming to the startling realization that this kind of thing might happen A LOT MORE than we all think. Think of how many flights there are in the world every single day. And think about how many business people take the same flights to and from meetings and international offices . . . Honestly, the world is going mad. Soon you'll be on a flight that's about to land and you'll hear:

'We are about to begin our descent into our destination. Please make sure your window blinds are open, your tray tables are up and your tits and cocks are safely lobbed back in your pants. Thank you for flying Sleazy Jet.'

My greatest complaint perk happened that fateful time I was wrongly arrested in a hotel in my underpants. Oh, you weren't aware of this? Well then, allow me to elaborate . . .

Oooh, I love this story.

I was on tour in 2016 and after a Sunday-night tour show just north of London, I travelled to a hotel in central London to stay over in preparation for my Monday-night show in a West End theatre. I checked into the hotel at about midnight. The staff were VERY weird with me; they were looking at me strangely and asking me a lot of odd questions. Where had I been, how long was I staying, where was I from? Usually staff at midnight on hotel receptions don't even look you in the eye. But I'm used to a bit of extra attention, being a Z-list celebrity, though it's usually in the realm of 'Where do I know this northern prick from?!'

I went to my room and began to unpack, I was there for two nights so (and this is tragic, I know) I got to actually take things out of my suitcase and hang them up in the wardrobe AND unpack my toiletry bag and line up all the little bottles and things on the bathroom counter. It's the little things in life, guys.

I hate that you do this. It's literally midnight and you're lining up all your toiletries above the loo? How can you be arsed?!

Now, I undressed to my boxer shorts and sat on the bed with my laptop . . .

Oh aye . . .

. . . joined the free wi-fi and . . . well, come on. It's midnight, I'm on tour in a hotel by myself and the wi-fi is good . . . Do I need to spell this out for you?

Did you YouTube hotel unpacking vlogs? Seems to be your thing.

Well, just as I opened a particular video-based website (call it a hub?), there was a knock at my hotel door . . . a loud knock.

I closed my laptop faster than a teenager who has just heard his mam coming up the stairs. I stood up and walked to the bottom of the bed while looking anxiously at the hotel door. I hadn't ordered any room service, I hadn't left any bags at reception for a porter to bring up or anything . . . so I quietly said, 'Hello?' and got the reply, 'It's the police, open the door!'

I obviously didn't believe them so I laughed and said, 'WHAT?!' At which point the door was opened and kicked in! However, this particular hotel has INCREDIBLE safety latches on the doors so the door was violently kicked in three whole inches . . . then a collection of gloved hands came through the opening and desperately grasped at the air trying to find the latch while multiple male voices shouted, 'OPEN THIS DOOR! IT'S THE POLICE!' It was at this point I fully believed it was, in fact, the police.

I didn't know that it only opened three inches! That's hilarious. Imagine how gutted they must have been.

I shouted, 'THE LATCH IS ON!', and ran to open the door for the increasingly angry male voices. I started to push the door closed and they started screaming and shouting as if I was attempting to lock them out again. I shouted back, 'THE LATCH IS ON!', they shouted, 'OPEN THE DOOR!' I shouted, 'I NEED TO CLOSE IT TO TAKE THE LATCH OFF!' There was a moment of silence as I closed it, removed the latch, then opened it fully.

(Fuck me, can we just appreciate what a latch it was! 10/10, would recommend to a friend.)

The silence was broken by the sound of angry kerfuffling as three policemen exploded through the narrow doorway shouting, grabbing me, restraining me and, let's be honest here, probably all thinking, 'Fuck me, that was a strong latch!' They put my arm up my back and pinned me face first against the wall while they put handcuffs on me and told me I was coming with them. They just kept saying, 'You're coming with us!' My mind was racing. For these first few seconds I was split between three things:

1. Holy shit, I'm being framed for a crime! I've just watched *Making A Murderer* on Netflix, I'm going to jail for eighteen years!
2. This is a prank.
3. These strippers are rough . . . and they're all men!?

Merry Christmas!!!!

I was walked out into the corridor in handcuffs and underpants (amazing title for an autobiography – if you're a male stripper reading this, you can have that – YOU'RE WELCOME, MATE!) and I was half laughing but I could feel a cry coming on, the kind of frustration, embarrassment and tears you had to hold back when a teacher at school shouted at you in full view of the entire class. I kept saying, 'What have I done?!' And they just kept saying, 'YOU'RE COMING WITH US!' It was terrifying. I only wanted to have a cheeky wank to get myself to sleep after a day of touring and travelling and now I'm being paraded down a hotel corridor in my boxer shorts . . .

My mind was racing. Time slowed down. What had I done?! Why was this happening? WAIT. That's it! They must have the wi-fi in the hotel monitored. I use a VPN sometimes to bypass hotel firewalls and watch American TV shows on UK internet. Shit, they knew. What did they think I was up to?! I stopped walking for a second, holding back tears and, in all honesty, holding back what must have been a gallon of piss that was attempting to leave my body in this fight-or-flight scenario, and I shouted in the hotel corridor, in my boxer shorts and hand-cuffs, 'IT WAS NORMAL PORN!'

They stopped walking. They looked at each other for a moment. They looked at me. Then one of them said to the others, 'OK, guys, I think we've made a mistake here . . . Take him back to his room.' And they marched me back to my room, sat me on the bed, took the handcuffs off and explained to me what had happened.

Earlier that day, a man had randomly entered the hotel from the street. He had been verbally abusing the staff with racist slurs then produced a knife to enhance the threats. The man fled when he heard the police were on their way. They never caught him.

I checked in, twelve hours later. And apparently I matched the description of this bloke?! This knife-wielding, racist maniac who by all accounts must have been VERY IMPRESSED with the look of the place because, while throwing around racial slurs and brandishing a knife, he clearly thought to himself, 'THIS IS A NICE HOTEL, I'LL BE SURE TO CHECK IN HERE FOR A SLEEP WHEN I'M DONE WITH ALL THIS TOMFOOLERY! HOPE THE WI-FI IS GOOD!'

Ridiculous. I didn't match his description at all. I can safely say I bet I looked FUCK ALL like the guy. I guarantee the poor, traumatized staff were just looking at me, thinking, 'Where do I know this northern prick from?!'

So they put 2 and 2 together and came up with 658 (my room number) and subjected me to some handcuff and underpants trauma of my own.

The police were very nice in the end – one of them even handed me a robe as they were explaining all of this to me. He couldn't quite hide how much he was laughing, but hey, I'm a stand-up comedian, a laugh's a laugh!

When they left I opened that minibar and inhaled the contents to calm myself down. I phoned my support act Carl Hutchinson, who came down to my room and drank with me as I told him the horror of what had happened.

Now I'm sure I don't have to explain what my complaint was about. So the hotel were VERY apologetic. The next morning I was treated to the same level of ass-kissing that Kevin McCallister receives the morning after the hotel staff THINK they have walked in on his father (inflatable clown) in the shower in *Home Alone 2: Lost in New York* . . .

'GOOD MORNING, MR McCALLISTER! Here's your limousine and your pizza!'

I felt like a god. Albeit a god who everyone knew had been crying in the hotel corridor in his underpants eight hours earlier.

The minibar was free, the two-night stay was free. The breakfast the next day was free and the suite that myself and Rosie stayed in a few months later in that very hotel was also FREE!

Not that Rosie deserved it, to be honest, because when the police left my room and I was in a tearful, shaky state, just before I phoned my support act Carl, I phoned my dear wife to confide in her, but she was pissed and just laughed then said she couldn't hear me and hung up. So that was nice.

When will you forgive me for this? I THOUGHT YOU WERE JOKING!

Even so, I think I'd still rather go through all of this than see a bloke get his nob AND BALLS out in the next row on my flight. Seriously.

Are We Vanilla?

In the time since starting the podcast we have been absolutely inundated with so many questions and stories from our incredible (and let's be honest, fucking disturbed) listeners.

We get a lot of sex-related horror stories and they almost always result in me shouting my now catchphrase: 'What is wrong with everyone?!'

(Truth be told these are always my favourite.)

I often hold back saying it as sometimes the podcast would just be me shouting that for an hour. People blow my mind.

But the more I think about the question 'What's wrong with everyone?!' the more I am starting to think that maybe it's not them – maybe it's us. Are we just boring when it comes to stuff like that? Are we repressed and vanilla? I'm not going to give you a step-by-step rundown of our sex lives here, but I can safely say that I don't think either of us is secretly crying out for the other to do some weird fucked-up stuff to the other . . . I think one of us would have blurted it out while drunk by now, and we'd either be currently doing it, or ripping the piss out of the one who said it on a daily basis.

'I'm sticking the coffee machine on, do you want one?'

'Yeah, please.'

'Milk and two sweeteners?'

'Yeah, thanks.'

'. . . want me to stick my toes in it too, you fucking pervert?!'

'I WAS DRUNK!!'

Threesomes and sex toys are one thing, but some of the stuff . . . it just seems like so much effort. Do these people ever just have a 'quickie'? Or do they always have to have forty-five minutes' prep time of getting the torture rack out and freezing a bit of human shit in a condom or whatever the fuck first?

The main thing that bends my head is how do they know these particular weird things turn them on, and how do they first broach it with a partner?

Take this, for example:

Good day, Chris and Rosie,

When I was 18 I got in my first relationship. And to say our sex life was very basic was an understatement. Very vanilla.

Apart from one thing she liked. When we would be in the bedroom, we would just stick to missionary and that was it. Being an 18-year-old lad, I thought this was normal.

But my girlfriend had a Jacuzzi bath and sometimes we started to fool around when both in the bath. This is where the interesting twist occurs. She would love and I mean LOVE to get me to pull her hair and hold her head under the water while having sex with her. Struggling to breathe and leaving it to the last possible second to slap my leg which was a code to pull her up, she would get her breath back quickly and request I do it again.

Ever since then I thought that was a normal kink, but as the years have gone by and with the conversations I have had, I have discovered this is a weird kink.

Louis

YES, IT'S PROPER WEIRD!! You were almost drowning the girl at her request – it's off-the-scale weird, not to mention dangerous as fuck . . . and this is one of the TAME emails we get . . . I'm building up to the messed-up ones, strap yourself in.

How do you realize that suffocation is your thing? Have an asthma attack during sex?! Finger yourself during a house fire?! And more importantly . . . did this lad attempt it with his next partner, thinking it was normal, and did she phone the police?

I think fingering yourself during a house fire is possibly the worst thing you've ever said. Bravo! You've done it.

'WHAT THE HELL ARE YOU DOING!?'

'Sorry, I thought this was what you do in the bath.'

'YEAH, IF YOU'RE TRYING TO MURDER SOMEONE!'

I mean, at least they were in a relationship, but some of the mad bastards attempt these twisted things after just a few dates or even on one-night stands! How confident do you have to be to let someone into that side of your personality when you probably aren't 100 per cent sure what their surname is?

You ready for a weird one, dear reader? A REALLY WEIRD ONE . . .

They might be but I'm not sure I am.

Dear Chris and Rosie,

There was a sexual interaction I was unfortunately involved with when I was young and dumb that I need to tell you about. The guy seemed perfectly normal and so has contributed to my lack of trust in humankind in general. We had a couple of dates before we decided to 'buck'. We went back to my flat where I lived alone (first mistake) and went to the bedroom. Everything was progressing well until he told me he was into S and M. I am fairly well versed in mild kinks so this was no problem for me. I was thinking it would be a bit of blindfolding and spanking to start, seeing as this was the first time we were trying it and didn't know each other's limits yet. But no. He pulled a dog collar and lead out of his bag. Bit presumptuous, but maybe he likes to be the sub and wear a collar, which I would be OK with. But no. The collar was for me. He said he had 'guessed my size' from our previous dates and bought it especially for me. I wish so much that I had made him leave there and then. But I was young and insecure and grateful for any attention given. So I agreed to have the collar but refused the lead. Weirdly, the collar was a perfect fit. So maybe he's not new to guessing neck size.

I won't go into details but at one point I was told to get on my hands and knees and bark because 'that's what bitches do'. That was my limit and I told him to leave. He was more than happy to leave, took all his stuff but left me 'my' collar.

I never contacted him again and he didn't contact me and till this day I'm still not sure if it was a strange fever dream.

Anon

WHAT THE SHIT?! I could write an entire book about this one story. Holy fuck.

(Shagged. Married. Annoyed. 2: The Collar.)

Just to pick a few highlights:

'I'm fairly versed in mild kinks' – it's this kind of sentence that makes me believe that it's me who is a giant prude and everyone else out there would be well up for giving or receiving a donkey punch from someone during sex. What is wrong with everyone?!

See this quote here to me screams, 'I've only had three sexual partners and they were all deviants so I don't know any better. I've also grown up in a generation where porn is freely available and I don't realize that sometimes it's just nice to have really good, really sensual, plain in-and-out sex with someone who loves me.'

'I was thinking a bit of blindfolding and spanking' – I've always been fascinated with the blindfolding thing. I don't think I would be able to take 'This would be so much better if I couldn't see you AT ALL' as anything but a massive kick in the balls (not the S and M kind). What is WRONG with EVERYONE?!

That's a shame because I'd be really up for that, to be honest, especially once this book's done.

'He said he had guessed my size from our previous dates' – AND IT FIT! Jesus Christ. He's a killer. An actual killer. He stared at her neck night after night and measured it with his eyes, then went to a sex shop (or a pet shop . . . dunno what would be worse) and picked one out with her in mind. HE IS A MURDERER. WHAT IS WRONG WITH EVERYONE?! (Just realized he could actually be a tailor, but I'm past the point of accepting that.)

I agree with the first option here, this man is most definitely not a tailor.

'. . . at one point I was told to get on my hands and knees and bark because "that's what bitches do".' I'm so glad this was the straw that broke the camel's (or dog's?) back. I just can't get over the fact that it got this far. Bless this poor woman. And I think that's what these perverts do . . . they prey on people who are too polite. It seems to me, a mixture of too polite and too horny could get you in a fuckload of trouble. Thankfully I'm a bit of a prick so I'd be fine in this situation.

My only question now is, does she still have the collar?

You know he only left it with her in case she changed her mind, right? I bet he's got a deal going with the sex catalogue people. Buy ten get ten free or something like that. He probably tries it with every girl he meets online. What's that saying again? Throw enough shit and some sticks? He's thinking she's going to ring him back one day and say, 'You know what, it chafed at first but I've really grown quite fond of this collar. Fancy coming round and we can do that barking stuff again?'

I have to say, as disgusted as I am, at least this pervert – who is DEFINITELY on some kind of list that the RSPCA have banning him from owning a dog and going within 500 yards of Crufts (probably isn't even allowed to watch it on TV) – asked her if she would participate, and told her his perversion. Sometimes these poor people get it sprung on them . . .

This is HORRIFIC. You have been warned.

Oh Lord . . .

One of my friends had matched with a guy on Tinder, they had been on a few dates and everything was going well. The guy asked her round to his house on their third date where he was going to cook her a meal, chicken dinner, her favourite. She agreed, went round to his house the following weekend and he cooked for her. After they had finished the meal they both started to have agonizing stomach pains, there was a race to the toilet and the guy won.

After being stood in his living room for ten minutes her bowels finally gave in and she shat in her pants, down her trousers and on his kitchen floor.

After he came out of the bathroom he was very understanding. He told her to get a shower, clean herself up and he would put

her clothes in the wash which she thought
was lovely.

After cleaning herself up and walking out of
the bathroom into his bedroom, she couldn't
believe her eyes. The guy had all of her
shitty clothing rolled up into a ball and
was rubbing it over his naked body.

Turns out the guy had a shit fetish and had
FED her a laxative.

Please don't mention my name as I do not
know this girl and would hate for her to
think I was stealing her story.

Anon

Told you. Told you it was the worst.

I can see it, Chris. I can see him lying on the bed in my mind!!!

I mean, I barely know where to start with this one. He should be
in prison, right? We are all agreed on that, yeah? Good. I'm not
sure what the charge would be ... 'Drugging someone with
laxatives then stealing their poo' doesn't have that legal ring to
it, does it? I don't know, I'm not a lawyer.

I absolutely LOVE the fact that he took the laxatives himself
too! What dedication to your perversion. I'm almost impressed.
Then he raced her to the toilet and sat there until he knew she'd

shat herself. OR he didn't take them himself and he just went and sat on his phone in the toilet until the poor girl couldn't hold it any longer. Either way. Prison.

I absolutely do not believe that he took any of those laxatives himself. It was all just a ruse to get the poor lass to empty herself, and on the kitchen floor too! Where food is prepared! Bless her heart though, she must have been mortified. I personally think I would have left there and then. I'd have nicked a towel from the bathroom, let him keep all my clothes and called food hygiene services as he deserves a one star for sure.

I do have one small question . . . Do laxatives have a taste?

Well, I've googled it and apparently a lot of them don't if you mix them with liquids – that's how the sneaky little trickster got away with it in the first place. What a way to ruin a lovely chicken dinner – he wants to be locked up for that alone! Bloody sacrilege!

I have tried laxatives myself before, when I was younger – probably only 10 or 11. We found some of my friend's mam's laxative chocolate bars in her bedroom. Yes, we were rooting around in her mam's bedroom. Looking back now, totally not OK. I have no idea what we were looking for and I know it was never my idea.

We all used to do it all the time. Unfortunately for this book, nothing very exciting ever came of it. We'd sometimes find a few quid in a dad's jacket or the odd bit of old make-up that we'd nick, but nothing more sinister than the laxative chocolate bar. But let this be a warning to you all now . . . Hide EVERYTHING. Teenage children will snoop around your possessions with their friends. They'll find stuff you probably forgot you had. Make sure you know where everything is . . . (I'm talking about your vibrators, lasses. Hide your vibrators.)

Back to the chocolate. We all had a few squares – it was vile. I remember the chocolate not being brown; it was mostly white with little air bubbles all over it. We were giggling so much that if we did happen to shit ourselves I reckon it would have been through laughing rather than the actual chocolate bar itself.

Nothing happened. I don't think we actually had enough of it to do anything, to be fair, and it was most definitely out of date.

My friend did take it one step further, mind, and sat on the loo pretending to squeeze a poo out. Very funny indeed. In fact, I have never thought about that day until this very moment, and it was extremely funny, albeit a bit rank – but those summer holidays were long! You had to find enjoyment where you could. Plus this was long before iPads and social media. These were the days when your hours would be spent learning dance routines by watching STEPS videos on The Box. Good Lord.

Right, now I can't be having you lot thinking that it's just blokes who do all this freaky kind of stuff . . . It's currently 2–1 to the perverted men, so here you go . . . Don't worry, this one isn't as bad. Sadly, the men do steal the trophy for 'Most Stomach Turning Perversions'; I can't defend that. This next one is just a bit strange . . .

Hi Chris and Rosie,

Me and a group of friends were sitting in a pub one night, having a catch-up with a few drinks as you do. After a few drinks we somehow got on to the topic of weirdest one-night stands.

We all traded stories that we had experienced, leaving just one friend left who was hesitant to say his. You'll understand why when you read on . . .

He explained that he had matched with a girl on Tinder and had gone for a drive only to end up going back to hers. One thing led to another and things started heating up before she stopped and told my friend she liked things done in a particular way and she would only carry on if he agreed to her T&Cs.

She wouldn't tell him what she liked done but he agreed nonetheless.

Once he agreed she told him to make himself comfortable on the bed while she went to the bathroom and sorted herself out.

A few moments later the bathroom door opened for him to be presented with nothing more than her in a cat costume, crawling on all fours and meowing at him. It wasn't until she got on to the bed that he realized that there was no going back, so he did what he had to do to get out of the situation . . .

Needless to say, there hasn't been a gathering where this isn't brought up to embarrass him in front of a new girl he is dating.

Jordan

OK, first question . . . What kind of cat costume? Are we talking Michelle Pfeiffer in *Batman Returns* or James Corden in *Cats*? I'm no latex fiend, but I can absolutely say hands down I would prefer the former.

I'd be scared if someone came out in a colourful, fluffy cat costume looking like they were going to a kids' fancy dress party. Think of how warm you'd get! And think of washing it after . . . at least the latex is wipe-clean!

I also have to say to the person who sent us this story . . . your mate LOVED it. He is pretending he didn't, but I'm telling you he did. Because there is no way that the only way out of that situation was to have sex – he could have just left. Verbal contract or not. What's she going to do? Sue him? Give him a bad rating on Tinder? (I've never used it but it's like Uber, yeah?)

So you are right, in my opinion, to keep taking the piss out of him. You need to order a saucer of milk to the table every single time you are all in the pub together. Literally every time, it'll never get old. I promise.

He absolutely loved it.

I can happily say I haven't been asked to do any weird shit in the past, thankfully, because I would have just laughed. Or got really scared and left. I remember a girl once said, 'Talk dirty to me', and I just drew a blank and stayed quiet. It was really awkward. You have to give someone warning! You can't just blurt that out randomly. I wasn't ready, I had no material prepared! I honestly can't think of any other weird stories . . . Maybe I've blanked them out?!

ANYWAY . . . I'm hoping you're all just as disgusted by all of this as I am (and I know Rosie is).

Disgusted, yet not surprised.

So I suppose that gives me a little hope that we're not the weird ones? Surely?

Yes, we may be a BIT vanilla, but vanilla is my favourite flavour! I love vanilla, I love a plain cheeseburger, I like a plain sponge cake, my favourite pizza is marguerita. Just plain old cheese and tomato. I always get laughed at when ordering pizza in a group, then I look at the car crash of a pizza that other people order . . . 'meat feast' and that kind of thing. Half a bloody farmyard on top of your pizza and an oil slick left in the box after . . . and have you ever seen someone successfully get the entire slice in their mouth without most of the toppings falling back into the box?!

OK, I've just realized that the analogy fell apart and I'm just taking about pizza now . . .

What I'm trying to say is, sometimes the most basic flavours are the best, you can enjoy it more. And doesn't it just mean that you enjoy each other without any extra crap being involved? Just the two of you. I think that when you have to add blind-folds, whips, fire, dog leads and human waste, where the hell does it end? What happens when you get sick of that? Strap your dick to a firework and shoot it into someone's bum? Oh God, I've just given someone their new kink, haven't I? Shit.

Married

Stags and Hens

While I love stag dos I really can't think of a more depressing place than strip clubs! However, I was at one a few years ago on a stag do, and we decided that we would all get a lap dance and get the stag one. Having never had a professional lap dance before, I didn't know what to do or where to look, so settled for looking across the room at the groom-to-be, who was looking just as uncomfortable as I felt!

During the dance, the lady leaned in and whispered into his ear, which made him pull a look that was equal parts disgust, shock and a little amusement. Once we were back in the bar I asked him what it was that she had asked, and honestly, if you'd given me the rest of my life to guess, I would never have come up with the answer. He told me she leaned in and whispered, 'If you want, I can fart in your eyes!!'

So I have a few questions. Firstly, did she just have one brewing and thought she could

use it? How often does this get requested
that she has started offering it as a
service? Finally, how much of a rotten
pervert does my mate look for her to think
he'd be into it? (Honestly, he's a clean-cut,
good-looking lad!)

Chris

Well, can I just say, I too would have never in a million years
guessed that was what she said! Part of me thinks maybe your
mate misheard because of the loud music in the club, but we've
been getting stories like this from the public for so long now
that I honestly believe that is what she said.

Part of me hopes that it's something her and her stripper
mates say to freak blokes out, but I know for a fact they would
get a huge hit rate of blokes who'd be up for it!

She meant it.

It's gross.

And I would be interested to know how much extra that
costs and if she would have gone to a private room to do it?

I've recently had conjunctivitis and I can tell you it's no laughing matter. It was an extremely mild case which lasted less than
forty-eight hours. This place should be shut down immediately.
I don't think your mate looks like a pervert, I just think perverts
come in all shapes and sizes these days . . . I hope it didn't ruin
his stag do.

I personally absolutely hate strip clubs, and that's not because
I'm writing this in a book WITH my wife – I honestly hate them.

I have no idea how they are still a thing. I have no idea why blokes enjoy going there. I cannot be comfortable in a room where I know most of the men there have full-blown erections. I've been to strip clubs in the past. Firstly, out of curiosity, then because everyone else on the night out is going, so you have to go or sit in the next bar on your own.

I never know how to act in these places. If you act like you hate it, I feel like that's a massive 'fuck you' to the staff. But then, if you're absolutely buzzing and loving your life to be there, you feel like a pervert. I don't know where to look, I don't know where to put myself, I don't like it at all.

All of my mates went to one while we were at uni and I watched a friend of mine (who didn't have much money) get three, that's THREE private £40-a-pop dances from a girl there. He went back to the booth again and again and again. He came back to the table absolutely beaming: 'She's on my course at uni! We're going to meet up next week!' She wasn't, and they never did. But to this day I respect her tactic for ripping off perverts.

'What do you do, love?'

'I'm at uni.'

'Me too!'

'Which one?'

'Newcastle.'

'Me too!'

'What course?'

'<insert subject here>'

'Me too! It's £40 a dance by the way.'

Genius. I still wish he'd quizzed her about certain aspects of the subject, but I don't think there was much blood in his brain at the time . . .

When I booked my stag do to Portugal, I told all of my mates that under no circumstances at all were we to go to a strip club on the holiday or any of that disgusting stag-do crap. No strippers, no getting all my clothes taken off me, no being handcuffed or tied to anything or ANYONE or any horrible shit like that. I was TERRIFIED that they would do something horrendous, just to upset me, so I genuinely went out every night in Portugal with about 500 euros as bribe money to pay off anyone who had been hired to come and ruin my night.

Chris, you've made your point. You're a good husband. Well done.

And I'm not alone. A mate of mine once SPRINTED out of a bar, down the street and continued for about a mile à la Forrest Gump when he got to a pub on his birthday night out and realized that everyone had booked a stripper for him. I've never seen anyone run so fast in my life. It was genuinely impressive. By the time everyone got down the stairs and out of the door after him he was a speck on the horizon.

I'm sorry if this is all sounding a bit laddy, I'm really not trying to be. I wouldn't consider myself a LAD by any stretch of the imagination, but as soon as you mention 'stag do' everyone paints that picture in their heads. My stag do was just a holiday but with excessive alcohol consumption. It was basically what I had always expected a 'lads' holiday' to be like, but up until that

point 'lads' holidays' had been when I was a teenager and it basically consisted of being scared all day by the bigger boys at the
pool, then going out and either ending up unconscious or looking after your unconscious mate. Absolute disasters. But my stag
do was just so much fun! Everyone who went on it still talks of it
to this day like, it's the stuff of legend! It really annoys Rosie.

He's right – they do and it does. My dad mentions it every
time I see him. I have also overheard Chris suggesting doing it
again and him paying for everyone. Not happening.

I must give the masses what they want!
    A few things happened that would make it legendary in my
eyes. Firstly, there were no randoms on it. Ladies, you might not
know this, but for some ridiculous reason, some blokes will go
on ANYONE'S stag do. Literally anyone. Friend of a friend of a
friend of a friend.

It's because of the strippers, Chris.

'Oh, is there a stag do happening? What's the dates? I'll book it
off work now!'
    'Errm, no, mate, you must have misheard . . . Now can I have
a Big Mac Meal with . . .'
    But mine was just people that I knew REALLY well, so already
I knew no one was going to be a liability . . . but then again,
when we landed in Newcastle we did have to drop three guys
straight off at the hospital.
    Here's why . . .

My brother-in-law broke his ankle on the second day and just decided to hobble around for the remaining two days rather than go to the hospital . . . I don't think he had insurance.

He definitely won't have had insurance.

He was climbing over the fence of the hotel to go to the shop as he wanted to avoid walking the long way round through reception. He scaled what must have been a ten-foot metal fence while me and everyone else shouted, 'DON'T, MATE! JUST WALK AROUND, YOU IDIOT!', then to our collective surprise he landed on the other side with perfect form. Tens all round from the judges! Then he took a bow, turned to walk away and fell down what must have been a four-inch kerb on to the road and broke his ankle. Moron.

Another lad (they will all remain anonymous as I can't be bothered with the legal ramifications of naming people in a book, plus they are all an embarrassment and I don't think they should be given any attention) dove into the pool in the exact spot where the shallow end turns rapidly deep . . . meaning, there is an underwater steep drop on the floor of the pool. He was airborne over the deep end but crashed head-first (nose first) directly on to the lip of the drop. Like smashing your face on the top of a ramp. He broke his nose. THEN he went under an umbrella to have a sleep, which is always a BRILLIANT idea when you have just taken a blow to the head. However, his day got worse since he left his feet poking out of the shade and into the baking midday sun as he slept, and seeing as he is the

WHITEST MAN I HAVE EVER MET he ended up with second-degree burns on his feet. Again, moron.

The third little piggy was injured during a night watching an England Euro game that happened to be on while we were away. They scored and he ran into a dark, empty area of the bar to do his own little kick in celebration without realizing that the reason this area of the bar was empty was because it was a stage that you couldn't stand on as you would block the view of the screen for everyone else in the place. He smashed his shin bone directly off the sharp metal corner of the stage and opened a hole in his leg that looked like he had been shot. It ended up infected and finally ulcerated and genuinely still gives him a bit of bother to this day. I'd love to say, 'not his fault, it was dark, not a moron', but come on! They scored so you have to do a little kick yourself? Grow the fuck up. So again, moron.

Now, I'm sure you're all wondering – 'Come on, Chris, surely your mates did some kind of stag-do stuff to you? You must have been tortured by them in some way' – and you're right, they did, and to be fair, it was absolute genius.

Firstly, you might not know this, but I'm not really a huge football fan (see, not a LAD!). I was however up for watching the England game on the stag do because it was the Euros and that's what you do! My mates took this opportunity to pull off a beautifully subtle stag-do stunt. They dressed me head to toe in as much England and football memorabilia as you could physically fit on to a human. It was like a game of football Buckaroo! From the ground up they had me in:

- Football boots
- Shin guards (although I can think of someone else who needed them more than me)
- England socks
- England shorts
- England top
- Captain's armband
- England water bottle round my neck (which all of my drinks for the evening had to be in)
- Some kind of plastic clapper hands that I lost in the first bar
- St George's Cross face paint
- Red and white England wig

No, the genius behind this, if you haven't spotted it yet, is that when you see someone out handcuffed to an old man or naked taped to a lamppost, or dressed as a giant baby, you think, 'He's on his stag do, poor bloke!' When you see a guy on the night of an England Euro match walking along the road in Portugal wearing: football boots, shin guards, a full England strip, a captain's armband with his face painted in St George's Cross, a red and white England wig on and drinking all of his beer from an England water bottle, you think, 'He's a cunt.'

Agreed.

During one of the days in the hotel, there was another group of guys who were particularly loud and boisterous. They ended up smashing some furniture on their balcony, fighting with each other and causing a bit of a scene ... We were all genuinely mortified by this and they were all proper old men, which was weird. I'm not ageist, but I've never seen 60-year-olds fighting. It was like watching a nature documentary or something.

You've obviously never done a shift at an old people's home . . .

Anyway, later in the night we were all on my balcony (which was actually massive, as it went round on to the roof of the room below . . . it was like a giant dance floor!) and we saw the hotel staff walking near the pool with three armed police officers. They pointed up to us and began to walk towards our room. I knew what was happening. They thought it was us who had been causing all the trouble earlier on. It wasn't us. So I opted to go and intercept them on the way to my room and explain that we were not the guys they were looking for. Carl Hutchinson (my mate, support act and regular podcast fodder) was with me and he took it upon himself to lock both me and him out of the apartment by slamming the door behind us. Little did I know it was deliberate so that all the lads could get ready for my main stag-do surprise . . . he doesn't half pick his moments. As I stood there trying to open the door and knocking furiously the three policemen approached us and asked to be let in so they could talk to everyone. I began to explain to them that it wasn't us they were looking for when I was interrupted by the door quickly opening and then my mate who opened it running off back inside the room.

The cops put their hands on their guns.

Guns?? What the fuck.

Exactly. I assured them that it was all OK but they made me enter in front of them and we walked through the apartment towards the balcony. We turned the corner round to the giant dance floor roof thing and myself and three armed police officers were met by twenty-two of my mates all standing wearing CHRIS RAMSEY masks like some kind of cult. I'm still surprised I wasn't shot.

So four days of carnage, three armed policemen, a shitload of football memorabilia and a trip to A&E sums up my stag do . . . but at least no one asked to fart in my eyes.

Rosie, how was your hen do?

Firstly, I find it extremely heroic the lengths you have gone to to disguise the fact that you and your mates were clearly knee-deep in stripper clunge for almost a week. I just hope my dad wasn't with you.

He paid.

Secondly, you have possibly purposefully left out the fact that none of you, I repeat NONE of you, ever left the swimming pool for a piss the whole holiday. You drank cheap pints of lager, ate cheese toasties and pissed in the public hotel pool. Absolutely horrific. Some of you were married with kids at the time, I was mortified.

Now THAT is absolute bullshit! How dare you accuse me of doing such a thing on my stag do?! I would never . . . That was on Michael's stag do.

Thirdly, what happens on the hen do, stays on the hen do . . .

I'M KIDDING!! Imagine? Mind, my friend went on a hen do once when the bride-to-be gave a random guy a blow job. How grim is that? Not only was she due to get married, but who, no matter what their relationship status, is giving out blowies to strangers? Just blowies? Nothing else and nothing in return?! Eurgh!

I on the other hand was not dishing out the blowies.

I had a house party where I hired a cocktail waiter for the evening. We danced all night and sang on the karaoke in the garden. Then we went to the strippers. JOKING!!

To be totally honest with you, my hen do was pretty low key. I enjoyed it immensely. But back then I didn't need the excuse of a hen do to let my hair down. I had no kids, my money was my own and I had approximately 80 per cent less responsibility than I currently have. Other than the personal cocktail waiter and the sash I wore, it was pretty much like most of my Saturday nights out, to be honest.

Ask me what hen dos are like now and you'll get a completely different answer . . . I live for them! They're fucking AMAZING!! A few days away from my family, you say? Stay in a lush posh house, get as pissed as you can and not get woken up by a screaming kid at 6 a.m., you say? Said hen's mother and grandmother will make us all breakfast while we slob around in our pyjamas, you say? Prosecco pong and games on the lawn, you say? YES, MATE. Sign me up. I'll go on them all!

Genuinely sounds unreal, that. Can I come?

Plus None

I've been with my boyfriend now for over three years, we live together and are very happy. A few of my girlfriends are getting married this year and all of them have invited me but not my boyfriend to the weddings. They've met him numerous times and all get along whenever there are any get-togethers, so I'm puzzled as to why he wouldn't be invited with me as a plus one.

I understand there's a finance thing that comes with weddings, but I wouldn't dream of only inviting my girlfriend without her partner. To me, it's downright rude to invite one and not the other, especially as he gets on well with the soon-to-be grooms! The more I think about it, the more livid I get, and not only that, I HATE having to tell my boyfriend that I've been invited to yet another wedding but he hasn't. I feel so bad for him as he's now beginning to think it's got something to do with him, when I've been told that it's a finance thing.

Is this OK? How would you feel if this was
happening to you? How much of a commitment does
there have to be to be invited to a wedding?

Anon

I'm so, so sorry to be the person to tell you this, but your friends do not like your boyfriend.

Oh God, I knew you were going to say this. This is awkward . . .

They don't want to tell you as they love you, but they literally cannot stand him.

I feel sick . . .

This is the biggest day of their lives and they don't want your boyfriend there.

Let the ground swallow me up!

He'll be in all the pictures and they just don't want to live with the memory of it.

Photoshop is a hard skill to master, to be fair.

Harsh but true.

Sadly, I have to agree. Sorry.

Are your other friends' partners being invited? Because if they are then that is basically your answer right there (it will also make me feel a lot less guilty about telling you that your boyfriend is clearly awful – again, sorry).

Even if they're not keen on him they should still invite him – after three years together, he is a large part of your life. That being said, I've had to make similar sacrifices myself.

In all honesty, we didn't invite someone's partner and our guest got upset so we invited them anyway in the end. They split up for good almost instantly after the wedding. We'll never get that £100 back and they took a slice of cake home too.

Just one other thought though, has your boyfriend previously slept with ALL your friends? Making the whole having him at their wedding thing a bit awkward? Again *totally* speculating but . . . Could be the reason why.

Or tried to sleep with? Or tried to kiss? Or just generally letched on them in the past? We all know one of these guys . . .

Weddings are EXPENSIVE AF.

Think you know how much flowers are? Think again! It's unbelievable how many zeros are put on the end of price tags once they hear the W word.

I have a theory that just saying 'it's for a party' will save you some money . . . I'll try it at my next wedding.

Me too!

Then as well as the venue hire you have to pay for every person who attends lunch AND dinner. They also get a little present (favour) which has always struck me as strange. Every single wedding I've been to I've received a favour. Ask me where those favours are now.

Where are those favours now, Rosie?

No idea! Literally no idea where any of those favours are right now. I could search for a week and I wouldn't find them. What an absolute waste of money! We bought little boxes of posh chocolates for our guests, most were left on the tables – I spotted one in a bush outside the venue the day after. I think they cost about £400! I wish I'd never bothered. I want our downstairs repainted soon – that £400 would have come in lovely!

My tip: don't bother with favours. Unless you can be arsed to make them yourself (this is actually a huge pain in the arse, trust me). I decided about six months before our wedding that I wanted empty jars on our tables, wrapped with lace and filled with little tea light candles. Amazing, I thought, cheap as chips and they'll look bloody gorgeous. How wrong I was . . . We had to eat jarred food for months, the lace was extortionate and I burnt my fingers on the bastard glue gun. Ridiculous, looking back. Mind, they did look bonny on the day.

There were bloody glass jars ALL OVER THE PLACE for about six months. It was hell. The fridge was full of them as we desperately tried to consume enough jarred food to fill the tables. There were always some next to the sink waiting to be washed. Always a few on the drying rack on the other side of the sink drying off. And the garage was full of the bastards! Not to mention the bollocking I would get if I accidentally recycled one or, heaven forbid, bought something in a plastic container instead of a glass fucking jar!

Another bone of contention of mine is sweet tables. Why have sweet tables become a thing? They have bot all to do with a wedding, yet everyone seems to think they need one these days. Oh, and popcorn machines? I'm not being funny, but popcorn does not go with wine and that's all I'll be drinking come 1 p.m.

The same goes for photo booths. I mean, don't get me wrong – I have definitely enjoyed some drunken photo-booth moments with my besties, putting on random sunglasses and holding up signs saying 'Don't do it!', etc. But I can assure you if it wasn't there I would have had just as good a night.

Now, I know I sound like a complete scrooge and I promise you I'm not. I fell into this trap just like the rest of you. I thought my day wouldn't be special if I didn't have all of these things, like it was some sort of new tradition everyone had to adhere to.

For me, a photo booth is just forced fun. I hate them. Putting on silly outfits and getting your photo taken to look like it was a 'wacky night'. If you want your wedding to be 'wacky', put a free bar on and have a Jägerbomb fountain! Shit will get wacky, quick.

I just really don't like the pressure of it all. The keeping up with the Joneses element of weddings really upsets me.

It's sad, because a lot of people get themselves into huge amounts of debt for their weddings whereas others get help from parents, which is great, but not all of us are that lucky. We can't all expect to keep up with each other, can we? Honestly, some of the very best weddings I have been to have been in social-club halls filled with balloons, cheap drinks and good people. Recipe for success, in my eyes!

Thinking back, there were a couple of plus ones at our wedding that we didn't know yet, but it didn't really matter to me.

I was just happy to be getting married, and I was so drunk by the evening do that I had no idea who was there and who wasn't. A few weeks later I thanked someone for coming and they explained that they weren't there as they couldn't make it. I hadn't even realized.

I have no memory of anyone who was there after the ceremony . . . In some of the photos I actually look like a walking corpse. I regret nothing.

Chris was mortal by 4 p.m. Like slurring his words and shouting really loud.

I didn't mind, to be fair, as I was pretty pie-eyed myself. The part I did get a little bit frustrated with was our professional photographs . . .

We got married on a beautiful summer's day in 2014. It was actually the hottest day of the year, it was roasting. A lot of people got burnt and I was absolutely sweating my tits off. I decided not to get loads of group shots as I hate going to weddings and having to stand on steps for half an hour and shout 'Cheese!' and 'Sausages!' What are we? Nine? No, sorry again, Mrs Scrooge here, just not my bag.

My personal favourite is 'Can all the men walk towards the camera in a line and I'll take action shots?' Aye, watch *Reservoir Dogs* last night, did you, you unimaginative prick?

I asked our photographer to take natural shots of our guests during the day, then as the sun was setting Chris and I would sneak off into the grounds and get our photos taken together.

The sun began to set at about 8 p.m. It was really beautiful and so unbelievably warm. Chris and I were sozzled. We'd got a little carried away with the champagne and hadn't paced ourselves like we said we would – him more than me, might I add. But I was definitely three sheets to the wind.

My hair was a mess, I'd sweated 80 per cent of my make-up off and my dress was beyond scruffy. Annoyingly, while cowgirling the toilet (sitting the wrong way round as to be able to sit down properly) I had kissed my dress by accident, resulting in two great big lipstick-shaped stains right smack bang in the middle of my dress, right at the front. Great.

The photographer was waiting ready for us. OK, pay attention, Chris! Stop grinning like a Cheshire Cat. You look ridiculous!

I WAS HAPPY!

Halfway through and it wasn't going well. We were laughing like school kids and secretly I just wanted to get back to the party, sorry . . . wedding! Ha. Luckily, though, it did give us a chance to sober up a little. I fear that if we hadn't done them at this point we wouldn't have made it to the first dance.

Anyway, we're finally getting somewhere. 'I don't think these will look too bad, you know, babe,' I said to Chris.

'Rosie?'

'Yeah?'

'I've got a problem . . .'

'What do you mean, you've got a problem??'

'It's down there.' Pointing to his crotch.

'Eh? What you going on about?'

'I've got a semi on and I can't stand face on.'

'BAHAHAH!!' I couldn't hold it in and I burst out laughing in his face. The poor photographer didn't know where to put herself! Imagine the groom getting a bloody half erection while you're taking the most important photographs of their lives? It sums us up, to be honest. Of all the moments, Chris! To this day I still have no idea why it happened. Care to explain yourself, Ramsey? Or is it just because I'm so goddamn irresistible??

I say again, I regret nothing. I was holding my beautiful new wife in my arms, posing for photos, cuddling and kissing. Forgive me for being attracted to my wife! (I was hammered too.)

Truthfully, though, the only people who should really matter on the day are you and your partner. Everyone else is just an added bonus. Mind you, some people take their importance a little too seriously and start acting weird . . .

Hi Rosie and Chris,

My best friend has asked me to be her bridesmaid . . . We have been friends for over ten years and I was honoured to be asked.

Now, a week before the big day, my friend slipped into conversation that she will struggle to use the loo in her dress.

Having been a bridesmaid before, I was not surprised by this and assured her I would be there to help . . . She then went on to say she was worried she might need a nervous poo during the day and I may have to help wipe.

Is this asking too much? I'm not sure I feel comfortable wiping my best friend's arse and then going out and carrying on with a smile on my face! I also don't want to offend her. Please help! What would you do? What is too far?

Jemma

Now, big day bum-wiping . . . I have to say I 100 per cent agree with you that this is a big ask. It doesn't take much to shock me but that took me by surprise.

I just can't understand why that would enter her head, to be honest. Surely there's more important stuff to worry about than whether you can wipe your own arse on your wedding day? I mean, has she actually tried? How big is her dress, for God's sake? Does she have really little arms? I am flabbergasted.

I wonder whether your friend might be better placed asking a family member to undertake this task for her, say her mother or her sister, her grandmother or a close cousin perhaps?

Failing that, how about her new husband? Surely he's been in closer proximity to her arse than you have ever been? Then again, I don't know, you may be closer than I realize. I know that sounds really grim, getting your new husband to wipe you down after a shite on your wedding day, but it's 2020 and they are marrying each other. For better OR worse. You know what I mean? In sickness and in health . . . To forever wipeth thy bride's arse.

Mind, I do worry that your friend may have outrageously misjudged the roles a maid of honour should carry out. Has she ever been involved in a wedding before? It doesn't sound like it to me.

As I've been married once myself and played maid of honour at my sister's wedding, here's a quick little list of the 'assumed' duties of a MOH (got sick of writing it, didn't I).

- Organize the hen do.
- Make sure bride doesn't have food in her teeth.
- Keep bride's Prosecco glass full on the morning of the wedding.
- Tell bride she looks pretty even if she doesn't.

- Hold bride's dress while she walks down the aisle.
- Wipe bride's shitty arse?!?!?! **NO. It's not one of the jobs. It's absolutely not one of the jobs.**

My advice to you would be to agree for now that you will wipe your friend's bum for her on her big day, but when it comes to the actual day you will need to avoid ALL bathroom trips like the PLAGUE. If you see your friend giving you the eyes towards the bathroom look, you run. You hear me? Run.

Brides can be vicious. I've seen it myself first-hand. They are temperamental and extremely unpredictable, like a caged animal, some of them. You can see the hunger in their eyes. They've been thinking about this day for YEARS.

She is feeling so many emotions right now. There's panic, nervousness, fear, all those extra endorphins running around, and you need to watch out, because if she's not a very nice drunk then you are fucked, my love. To be honest, this is probably the most pivotal day for her to be wiping her own arse. She is officially a grown-up from today. No more messing about, no more holidays with the lasses, no more flirting with Sam from the office. Nope. She's married now. Taken. Joined. Attached. Trapped. Oh shit, did I say trapped?! LOL . . .

So, the only thing you can do is avoid her.

Obviously don't be a complete cow. You need to make sure you're there for the important stuff like the ceremony, photographs, speeches and the first dance and that, but honestly for everything else you just busy yourself.

Failing all of this, my last suggestion would be to slip her some strong laxatives on the morning of the wedding, get her good and empty before the ceremony.

Have a lush day. x

I've reserved comment until the end of this chapter as I am utterly shocked and appalled . . . I don't know where to start.

Firstly, I've always been confused by the fact that women wear shoes they can't walk or stand in for an entire night out that will involve a shitload of walking and standing.

But this?!

Look, wearing a dress that you have to take off to go to the toilet in, I can sort of get my head round. It's properly stupid though. Rosie sometimes wears jumpsuits that have to be removed and pissed around with (literally) in the toilet for hours. I can forgive it a bit more on a wedding day, I suppose . . .

This though?

Wearing a dress that you can't get out of, that you can't go to the toilet in – that you can't even wipe your arse in – is absolutely ridiculous. It can't be that nice a dress, it can't be worth it. Take it back and get another one, you filthy, filthy individual.

And let's finally tackle the issue of ASKING YOUR MATE TO WIPE YOUR SHITTY ARSE. I am furious on your behalf. Furious, mate. Does she want you to pop to the dress fitting and give it a little practice wipe?!

Can you imagine if this was a bloke?!

'Steve, do you want to be my best man?'

'It would be an honour, Gary.'

'Amazing, what a legend you are . . . Now, when you wipe someone else's arse, do you wipe front to back or back to front?'

'. . . What?'

FRIENDSHIP OVER.

Most blokes would draw the line at getting their mate's cock out and having to give it a little shake too, just so you know.

Holiday Friends

Whenever we go on holiday and my wife has
the audacity to speak to people around the
pool, I hate it and say, 'Don't speak to
them, don't think we're meeting in the bar
later or owt.' I think it's a pointless
exercise talking to folk we'll never meet
again, but she sees no harm in it. I see the
bigger picture. We'll never see them again,
so what's the point?

Tony

This is a hard one because I, like your wife, am a really chatty person. I really like meeting new people and having conversations. I'm also like you too, though, because the problem is I then don't ever want it to go any further than that.

A little bit of small talk on holiday is lovely; a night out with strangers? No, thank you.

I get this trait from my mother, who while on holiday would wear the biggest hat and make sure she had her head in a book 80 per cent of the day so that no one dared talk to her when she was around the swimming pool.

My dad, on the other hand, loved a bit of bants with the

other loungers. He'd often come back from the bar with strangers in tow and introduce them to my mam, then organize a meet-up later that evening around the pool bar after dinner. I distinctly remember my mam hollering at him upstairs in the room later on for bringing people over to chit-chat.

I never used to see the big deal when I was a kid. I thought it was quite nice that my dad was outgoing and enjoyed meeting new people. Now, though, as a grown woman I am a fully-fledged Sandra, with a degree in the form of resting bitch face.

I have to say, if I had a time machine, the first place I'd be going back to now is to one of those holidays just at the moment when Derek brings a half-pissed, day-drinking, pool bar bloke mate over to meet a bikini-wearing sunbathing Sandra . . .

'Sandra! Wake up, this is Phil . . . we're all going with his family tonight to an *Only Fools and Horses* themed pub to watch the Sunderland game!'

It has happened to us before, just the once mind.

We were on our honeymoon when we met a lush couple called Rach and Tim. They were staying in our hotel and, like us, they were a young couple enjoying a week away in the glorious Santorini sunshine.

We chatted in the pool and by the bar and even went out for a meal one night. What I liked about it was that it wasn't forced at all, we enjoyed each other's company and made it really clear that it was weird how much we all got on and that we understood if anyone was intruding on the other holiday, we could leave.

We honestly all said it every ten minutes, no word of a lie. It was our catchphrase!

We didn't spend every second of our time together but the times we did were very enjoyable. We're still friends on social media and I think about them every day. I don't, by the way – I'm joking.

I've got to be honest here. It was the fact that they had a suite with their own pool on the balcony that got me talking to them in the first place. I was literally only fishing for a shot in their pool . . . Annoyingly they turned out to be a lovely couple!

That holiday aside, I still don't go out of my way to make acquaintances on my jollies.

I used to work in a posh hotel in Rhodes back in the day. I witnessed lots of families and couples who would come back each year to meet the same families and couples. Problem being a lot of them couldn't stand each other but it had become so much of a habit that they felt obliged to turn up year after year.

Why would you put yourself through this? Also, why would you go to the same hotel year after year? Fair enough, the hotel I worked in was really nice, but go on, live a little!

I've been on Google and there are over 700,000 hotels around the globe – they could have gone ANYWHERE. Nope. Let's go back to Rhodes to spend time with the families we despise, all because you decided to chat to that daft sod when you went up for your all-inclusive beers fifteen years ago!

On the surface, Tony sounds like a right miserable prick . . . but I have to agree. It's not the initial chat, that's absolutely fine . . . It's that implied 'We chatted at the pool bar so we're best mates now!' mentality that I hate. Not everyone is as understanding as Tim and Rach. Some mates you make on holiday may even utter the dreaded phrase 'Let's meet up when we get back to England' – let's fucking not, eh?

Look, we've had a laugh, we were constantly drunk, the sun was shining, this isn't a real representation of who we all are as people. And to be quite frank, we all lower our mate standards so much on holiday, the very idea of taking these people back into the real world is absolutely terrifying. Imagine introducing them to your REAL mates? Your family? Imagine them staying at your house and using your towels on their arse? Exactly. Leave them. Give them a fake email address and get on the plane . . . And pray to God they are not on your flight.

However, I am a 'LONELY child', as Rosie calls it; I have no brothers or sisters and I only ever once took a mate on holiday. So my attitude to holiday mates has changed DRASTICALLY over the years. I'm going to admit it now before Rosie tells you all, I used to desperately attempt to make friends on holiday as a kid and my methods were utterly embarrassing . . . but they worked!

The one that gives Rosie the most joy is this one:

Hang around the pool area, either in it or by the side of it . . . (I have to say IN the pool works best as you can just stand there in the water and no one bats an eye that you're doing nothing but lurking) and keep on the lookout for two kids who are either already friends or usually siblings. Keep an eye on them and wait until they start to play any projectile-based game (bat and ball, passing the ball or frisbee, etc.).

Now unless you have the worst luck in the world and you have somehow picked the children of a top-flight tennis player or a family of travelling professional frisbee throwers . . . you're about to have yourself some holiday mates!

This is the most tragic story I have ever read. Oh God, there's more . . .

Stand near the worst catcher. You basically need to be next to the one who misses the frisbee the most, either because they just drop it a lot or because the kid throwing it to them is rubbish. Here comes the embarrassment . . .

Make it your job to fetch the stray ball/frisbee for them! LIKE A FUCKING WINNER!

Start by just getting it and then swimming over to the kid it was supposed to go to and giving it to them. THEN, soon, upgrade that to actually throwing it to them when you get it . . . THEN after a while, throw it BACK to the kid that threw it in the first place! After about fifteen minutes of this, they will just start passing it to you . . . you will be in the game via osmosis!

Eeeh, Chris. This is making me cry! But also cringe/laugh at the same time. Bless you, man.

Yes, it's pathetic, yes, it's weird, yes, you are sometimes laughed at and told to piss off, but MOST of the time . . . you have yourself the makings of a holiday mates gang!

YOU ARE WELCOME! (Probably doesn't work as well with adults . . . and don't use it with kids if you're an adult . . . that's just wrong.)

Other techniques I employed were:

- Hanging around the pool tables
- Hanging around the two-player arcade machines with a spare 25 pesetas
- Asking kids if they had seen my lost lilo (I didn't have one)
- Blatantly walking up to children and saying, 'Will you be my friend?'

The saddest thing about this whole story is that as a person with siblings I have witnessed children like yourself first-hand, desperately trying to encroach on our family game of piggy in the middle, failing miserably as it's only a game for three.

I wish that I knew then what I know now, as I'd have let you play with us for sure. Poor little lamb. I just want to let you know now, though, Chris, that siblings are honestly overrated. You can't stand the sight of each other until you're at least 22 and even then they can irritate the living shit out of you.

It might all look like fun and games on the surface, but if you delve slightly underneath that shiny exterior you can guarantee that one of them has probably thrown a remote control at the other around the breakfast table a mere hour previous (true story). Your parents argue more as they're stressed to bits. You never get new clothes. Oh, kiss your own room goodbye too! Vicious they are. Pure vicious. But yeah, in this case you do always have someone to play with, I suppose. Oh, and less responsibility once your parents are old and need caring for. You've got that little milestone to deal with all on your own, babe. Bless you, sweetheart. Maybe you could hang round the TV at the old people's home? See if anyone will play with you there? Worth a shot, eh?

Holidays for us these days are extremely different to what they were. Gone are the 5 p.m. gin and tonics round the adult pool, chilling in there until the sun sets, not a child in sight. Oh no, our holidays are now filled with endless hours of keeping a toddler entertained in the 40-degree sun!

We went to Greece a few years ago when Robin was one. We were all set for a lovely relaxing family getaway. The hotel we booked looked great, loads of stuff to keep us all entertained, the weather was set to be amazing and I personally couldn't wait to get there.

As soon as I started packing our suitcases I realized that this was a terrible idea. Unfortunately, it's not until you're packing a suitcase for a baby/child that you work out how many nappies they go through. Oh, my goodness! Why do they take up so much room? Forget about squeezing your hairdryer in the baby's bag, there's no bloody room! It's full of frigging nappies! Then there's formula, bottles, baby food/pouches, outfits, sun hats, toys, medicine, sun cream. They are so bloody high-maintenance.

Having not personally lifted a finger to help in the packing process, I can only describe my shock as the case was opened when we got to our destination and I genuinely thought Rosie had robbed Mothercare on our way to the airport.

Obviously we ended up using hardly any of it. Poor Robin used the same swimming trunks almost all week, bless him. Who has he got to impress? No one, that's who. Absolute waste of time.

Did I learn my lesson the year after and pack less when we went away? No, did I balls. If anything I packed more. Unfortunately, this is very much still a skill I need to master.

I'm an over packer, always have been. If you tell me I can take 30 kilograms then I will be using that full 30 kilograms no matter how long I'm going for. Two nights to two weeks, it's pretty much the same amount of shite going in there.

I brought back a half-empty bottle of Grey Goose and three cans of Diet Coke from a holiday once as they were quite expensive and I hate wasting things, so I thought, why not bring them home? I was over the weight limit so I got charged! It probably cost me more in charges than the actual bottle and cans were worth. Also, the bottle leaked in my bag so I didn't even see the fruits of my labour. Sad times.

You could enter that into some kind of sad short story competition and wipe the fucking floor with everyone, Rosie. Tragic that. I'm gutted for you . . . I mean, I would have been absolutely furious if I was with you!

We were on this particular holiday for a week. Chris always tries to get me to go for a fortnight but I just can't be away from home with a child for that long. Imagine what I'd need to pack! I'd probably try to take his bed! The weather prediction was correct and it was glorious. I swear, though, I came back paler than when I went. Little did I know that it's extremely difficult to catch those beautiful rays of sunshine while you're trying to get a screaming one-year-old to nap during the day, all so you can be in with the possibility of a few extra hours at the bar in the evening (terrible parents).

HEY, IT'S OUR HOLIDAY TOO!

He would not go to sleep during the day no matter what we did. He just would not nap. I would end up so stressed that he wasn't napping, I'd spend most of my afternoon rocking him back and forth under the parasol over our sun lounger. Making myself sick with worry that he was getting so out of his routine that when we got back home I'd end up with one of those children who just doesn't nap any more. I couldn't be having that! Those nap times are essential to my life!

I wish I was more relaxed when it comes to routine, I really do. I've always been a huge stickler for it, much to my own annoyance. I think that's why holidays always fill me with dread instead of excitement. The fear of not being surrounded by our own things, the fear of him not going to sleep at the right times and the knock-on effect it will inevitably have on the rest of our day.

I'm much better now that he's a bit older, but back then I was shocking. I've already vowed that with our next one I will be much more relaxed. I'll be that mam who is totally chill.

I'm not even going to keep check on naps. Just you wait! I'll be completely different . . . Ha! Who am I kidding? It made me feel ill just typing that!

Yeah, that was never going to happen.

I'm honestly really envious of those parents, the really relaxed ones. The ones who take everything in their stride. I've often seen them on days out – their children are whingeing or crying and they can ignore them. The incessant drivel and complaining just doesn't faze them at all. I want to be taught this skill, the I-don't-give-a-shit skill and you are not going to ruin my day. All Robin has to do is smile at me and I melt. That little shit has got us both wrapped round his little finger and the bugger knows it!

He currently has this little scheme going where he bats us off against each other, like a Mammy vs Daddy competition. He has learnt recently that if he says he likes/loves one parent more than the other it upsets us. Currently I am his main target. Daddy can do no wrong and Mammy is absolutely not his favourite parent. Shit on his shoe, you could say.

Chris pretends that it upsets him. He gives it the 'Ah Robin, that's not kind, Mammy loves you very much and you're making her very sad by saying that' treatment. But I know he is secretly LOVING it. He can't hide the little grin on his face every time Robin brings it up. I know your game, Chris, trying to make out that you're not absolutely buzzing to be Robin's favourite parent. Well, let me tell you, it doesn't last long. I'll give it two weeks tops before you're desperate for him to be all over me again.

It's not even going to take that long. I can't get a moment to myself!

Don't get me wrong, it's nice being Mr Popular for once . . . It's only taken me thirty-three years to be the most popular guy ANYWHERE, so I obviously enjoy it, but the added pressure of not being able to go for a shit without him asking where I am and coming in to watch is getting a bit much. You can have him back!

I thought I'd come up with a fail-safe plan to win Robin back for good. I decided I would use his cousin Abel as bait and tell Robin that he doesn't have to want to sit next to me or talk to me because I'm going to sit next to Abel instead. I'm going to make Abel's tea, I'm going to take Abel to the park and I'm going to play criminals with Abel. (Criminals is a game we all play together. It's a bit like cops and robbers, I'm always the cop and Robin and Chris are the robbers. Constantly outnumbered even in a fictional world.)

My plan didn't work. It failed that much that given the chance I think Robin would have quite happily put my coat and shoes on me and walked me round to Abel's house so him and his precious daddy can be alone together.

Will You Love the Baby
More Than Me?

Approximately three weeks into my third trimester after a little bit too much lager, Christopher Ramsey uttered these fateful words to a very pregnant and very hormonal me.

Yep. He did. He went there.

Chris – 'But Rosie, do you think you'll love the baby more than you love me?'

Me – 'Yes, Chris, I absolutely will.'

You see, unbeknownst to Chris, I knew I had this question coming.

A couple of friends of mine who were already mothers had talked of their partners asking the same thing.

Once he'd asked, there was no going back for him. The truth is I didn't even have to think about my answer. I knew from the minute I found out we were having a baby that the new ranking order in my mind and in our house would go . . .

1. Baby
2. Chris
3. Chocolate
4. Bed

I loved our baby growing inside of me more than anybody, including my husband who, let's be honest, at that point I still actually liked quite a bit. This was still very much in the no arguing phase of our relationship.

I have heard of women not answering honestly like I did and often telling their partners, 'Of course not! Of course I'll love you more! You will always come first, my darling!'

Eeeh, poor Chris, this is exactly what he wanted to hear that night as we lay in bed, him stroking my tummy, coming to the sharp realization that he was soon to be playing second fiddle to a 15-inch ball of flab. Little did we know though that little 15-inch ball of flab would soon become a 10-pound 11-ounces ball of absolute flab who would steal both our hearts and become the only number one.

Right . . . I feel I need to explain a few things here.

Yes, I asked that question. Not my finest hour.

Yes, I was pissed. But you know what? I would have probably asked that sober too . . . I think a lot of men would, and I'll tell you why.

I'm going to risk sounding sexist here . . . but I don't care, because I think I'm right.

Wow.

The majority of men are not made to have kids. We just aren't. We step up and learn to be fathers when the time comes, of course we do! But it's not something that is genetically in us. All we are really designed to do is dump our semen in any hole that will allow it.

The man I married, ladies and gentlemen . . .

Little girls play with dolls. Little girls play weddings. Little girls had that creepy board game growing up in the nineties where there was a phone in the middle and a load of cards with what were supposed to be sexy teenage guys but actually more closely resembled middle-aged men on them who you would call and they would give you clues as to which one had a crush on you and where to meet them . . . like some kind of paedophile roulette. (Yes, I know I know a lot about it – two girls lived next door to me when I was growing up and yes, I spent a lot of time playing this game. No, I didn't ever get the guy I wanted.)

It's called Dream Phone. And now you mention it, they were all really far too old to be hanging 'at the mall' . . .

My point here is, for the most part, in my experience, men are not prepared for anything as massive as having a baby any-where near as much as women are. And that's without taking into account biology. A woman literally has a clock ticking inside her (might not be an *actual* clock, I'll have to look it up) counting down to when she can no longer have kids, her body changes and the sex drive diminishes two to three times faster than a man's . . . I know this because I DID look this up, and I once saw a 70-year-old man watching Pornhub on an iPad on the train. I can't blame the guy, to be honest. Imagine living to 70 then dis-covering a never-ending library of HD, hand-held porn! I'm surprised he left the house.

It's not an actual clock, Chris, there's really no need to look that up.

I am generalizing here, and I know there are exceptions to this rule. There are of course women who absolutely do not want kids at all and there are blokes who say things like 'I can't wait to be a dad' out of nowhere to all the lads round the pool on the stag do and really bring the fucking mood down.

The moment Rosie saw that positive pregnancy test and knew that there was a baby growing in her stomach, that was it. It was real to her. She knew it was happening, she was overjoyed and head over heels in love with the little bump. It took a lot longer for me to accept this was happening and this was real. It wasn't as the bump grew, or the first kick, or even the birth . . . It was probably the first time I had to get up at 4 a.m. hung-over and make a bottle. That's when shit got real.

I'm not saying this is a macho man thing, far from it. It's an immaturity thing. I still sometimes look around for a real adult to come and help me in situations in life. I find myself looking at our son Robin now and again and thinking, 'Holy shit, I'm responsible for your entire life!' Rosie knew this from the moment she missed her period.

Our period! Haha.

My point here is, the kind of men who ask that question (and bloody hell, I thought it was only me who'd asked it until I read this so I'm buzzing about this whole thing now, in truth) are not mentally or emotionally prepared for a baby until the baby has

175

been around for quite a while. Yes, we instantly love and adore and want to protect the baby, but we would probably be happy letting someone else do all the heavy lifting, early mornings and feeds, etc., while we sit around waiting for cuddles and naps. And by someone else, I mean a stranger. I've heard Rosie in the past say things like 'I couldn't have someone else getting Robin ready for school or putting Robin to bed every night', whereas I'd already have an ad in the local paper if she was up for it.

What Chris is basically saying here is that he would quite happily hire a full-time live-in nanny, even though we both work from home and only have one child, who is at school.

I've got a theory that raising a child in a home is far too big a job for just two people. I have thought about this a lot and honestly believe the eighties film *Three Men and a Baby* was on to something. Three is the magic number.

Just picture it, with three of you in the relationship raising a kid, you could have a rota that caters to everyone's needs! It would be bliss.

Bath time? Two of you do it, one of you makes dinner!

Walk out to the park? Two of you go, one of you tidies the house.

Night feeds? Take one night each on a rotating basis. You will always get two nights in a row of uninterrupted sleep.

IT'S GENIUS!

Having been a father for four years now, I've almost come to terms with the immense responsibility and life-changing enormity of the whole thing. I can look back and feel a bit daft that I asked the question. In the cold light of reality, I can safely say I love him more than anyone or anything on earth. The things I would do to keep him safe are literally unimaginable. I would throw Rosie under a bus to save him, I would push her off a bridge to save him, I would set her on fire to save him, I would let her catch a bullet for him, I would throw boiling hot piss on her face to … Sorry, I'm getting carried away, you get what I mean.

I totally get her answer at the time now, and I understand her list. I don't mind at all that I come second to Robin, I'm just genuinely buzzing I came before chocolate, to be honest! Here's my list:

1. Robin
2. ~~PlayStation~~ Rosie
3. ~~Pornhub~~ Spending time with my family
4. Pizza

Firstly, Chris, your plan is completely flawed as there aren't enough bedrooms in our house for your three-parent plan to work. And if you think for one second that I'm sharing my bed with another grown adult and turning your little scheme into some sort of sexual/parenting fantasy of yours, then you are absolutely barking up the wrong tree, Mister! I've only just found out that my sex drive is diminishing by the day, I can't be adding more sex partner pressure on to myself like that!

It's strictly a sleeping thing. You know my opinions on threesomes!

Secondly, I'd rather you didn't, but if you ever do go through with the boiling piss in my face thing, please make sure to not use the new pan.

Deal.

Parenting Fails . . .

When I still lived with my mum and sister in my early twenties, I came home from work and my sister was home early from school. I asked her why she was home so early. The reason why she was home still shocks me now. She came home from school with a third-degree burn on her neck. This injury did not occur at school - it happened at home. My sister came down in the morning and said to my mum, 'My polo shirt needs ironing. Would you do it for me?' My mum was very happy to. But this is where the horror starts. As my sister starts taking her polo shirt off, my mum says, 'What are you doing?' My mum then grabs her still wearing the polo shirt and proceeds to iron it on my sister. As she's doing this, the iron automatically releases a massive burst of steam on to my sister's neck. This was in 2007 and I did a poll at work so I was well ahead of the time, and I can quite confidently say everyone at East Midlands Airport agreed that my mum is an absolute

nutter. The question is, have you ever done
anything questionable when parenting? I
highly doubt it will be as horrendous as
this.

Jimmy

I genuinely hope your sister recovered from her injuries and
that your mam managed to get away without a telling-off
from the social services for the accidental scalding. I'm hope-
ful that it was accidental?

I can only assume from your still very apparent horror
that you are without children currently? The reason I say this
is because your mam, God love her, albeit irrational and
extremely over-zealous with a red-hot implement, actually
reminds me of most mothers I know, including my own
mother and myself too.

Being a parent is horrific.

Not only do you have to care for yourself, you also have to
care for other little human beings, who believe me are not at
all capable of looking after themselves. As a parent, this can
put you in a lot of tricky and dangerous situations.

The A&E department of your local hospital will become a
much larger part of your life than you ever imagined. You
won't be alone either – often when you visit hospital with yet
another emergency, you will bump into friends with their own
children.

'He fell off the bastard bed!'

'She got her frigging finger trapped in the door!'

'He's got an inflamed ball and it won't go down!'

All true, by the way. Our home town, South Shields, is a pretty small place and the children's A&E is always pretty rammed. Especially on a weekend.

I know what you're thinking, Jimmy. 'How can you be so irresponsible? How can you not manage to keep your child safe??'

Children don't know what danger is, and sometimes when they do know what danger is, they sniff it out like a frigging basset hound.

My son has ZERO fear! Faced with the opportunity, he would throw himself off a cliff and think nothing of it. He can send an adult into a state of crisis with a simple outing to the local park. Potential danger lurks at every turn. I have more accident forms from his school than I do bank statements. The poor kid has no front teeth after one particular accident. That's how bad it got! He lost his two front teeth. The kid is TOOTH-LESS!!! I mean, that was my/Chris's fault, but it wouldn't have happened if he wasn't such a liability!

Basically, what I'm trying to say, Jimmy, is yes, your mother absolutely should not have tried to iron your sister's polo shirt while it was still on her body BUT I can totally see why she did it.

Now, strap yourself in for the tale of the fateful day when Robin lost his teeth . . .

It was a cold autumnal day in 2017. Chris was home and we decided to be insta perfect and take our little darling to the seaside.

Robin had just recently received a balance bike for his

birthday and he wanted to take it with us. He was two at the time so he didn't ask nicely, he just screamed at us for ten minutes before we begrudgingly put it in the boot of the car. Remembering his helmet, because 'safety first' (HA).

Now, as I mentioned earlier, Robin is unfazed by danger. So he was very fast on his balance bike and it was genuinely terrifying to watch him on it.

We found a little spot with a hill and Robin decided to go down it on his balance bike. Chris followed closely behind (Robin was going, like I said, VERY fast). Robin did this a couple of times and it was a bit, you know, dangerous. Chris suggested that maybe we don't let him do it again. I said, 'No, I think he'll be OK!'

SUGGESTED!?! You can piss right off, mate! I literally said the EXACT WORDS: 'Rosie, he almost fell that time. He's not going again, I can't keep hold of him, it's too dangerous.'
    And YOU blatantly said, 'Let him go again, it'll be fine!'

Biggest parenting mistake I have made. Ever. No, fuck that, it's the biggest misjudgement I have ever made in my entire life.

Yes, it was **YOUR** biggest mistake, Rosemary.

Third and final trip down the hill, our little innocent, darling 2-year-old son comes off his balance bike at what felt to me to be 100 mph, cracking his two gorgeous white baby teeth off the rock-hard pavement. Horrific. If I close my eyes I can still hear the noise they made hitting the floor.

Thank the Lord he had his helmet on as I honestly dread to think what would have happened if he hadn't.

Now comes the distressing bit (if that wasn't distressing enough).

Me – 'Oh, holy fuck! Chris!!! Why did you let him go down again?'

Chris –

Robin – 'WAAAAAAHHHHH! WAAAAHHHHH!'

Me – 'His teeth!!! OMG, Chris, his teeth!!! Go get the car!!!'

Chris –

I have deliberately left Chris's reply blank as he didn't say a single word during this entire time. He instead stood over us with his hand over his mouth like we had both been shot in front of him and were now being eaten by a pack of wolves.

Absolute sack of shit.

I think you're misremembering the facts again, my darling wife. I think you'll find I was crying uncontrollably and shouting, 'I TOLD YOU! I TOLD YOU!'

. . . Reading this back, I kind of think my version makes me sound like a bit of a wanker, so I'm happy to go with yours in the future.

Deal.

Chris is a wonderful father btw, which I'm sure I'll have mentioned at some point in this book (hopefully?) . . .

Literally the first and only time, but I'll take it . . . Might get this little bit of the book blown up and framed.

. . . but he is horrendous in stressful and upsetting situations.

To this day I am so mad at him for letting Robin go down for the third time.

Yes, I know I said he'd be OK but I don't know everything!! I'm not the bloody balance bike know-it-all oracle! He was the one running down with him, I think this lies at his door . . .

Sort of. OK. 50/50 blame? Please?

'Yes, I know I said he'd be OK but I don't know everything!!' This is an admission of guilt if I've ever seen one. I'll give you 70/30, best I can do.

Fast-forward slightly to a very speedy and frantic drive (by Chris) to South Shields children's A&E department.

We arrive, devastated by what has just happened. Covered in toddler teeth blood and absolutely riddled with parental guilt. The worst type of guilt there is.

The doctors and nurses were incredible. Robin was hard as nails and by this point he was Calpoled off his tits and laughing his head off as if nothing had happened.

It was pretty embarrassing that we were both in a worse state than him.

Chris couldn't look at him without crying, which irritated the fuck out of me, while I was trying to fabricate a story to the doctors that didn't make us sound like the worst parents on the planet.

At this point in the story Robin still had both his front teeth, albeit massively cracked. Unfortunately, though, a few months later one of his teeth started to die and go an off-grey colour.

Our dentist was on holiday at the time, so we were referred to the dental hospital. They told us that sadly they could not save Robin's dying tooth and that because he was still so young it would have to be removed. The other tooth was also extremely sketchy (they didn't use that exact terminology but that's basically what they were saying). Because of his young age they couldn't put him under anaesthetic twice, so they thought it best to just remove both teeth at the same time.

Obviously I'm not a doctor and know nothing about teeth, so I went along with what they said and understood that it needed to be done.

At a check-up with our dentist a few weeks after the operation and his return from his, might I just add, really fucking long holiday, he couldn't hide the shock on his face when he saw our little toothless Joe. He never said it out loud but I still to this day think that he could have saved at least one of Robin's teeth.

So, Jimmy, your poor mother made a grave mistake that day, a grave, silly mistake, but you need to forgive her as she's not unlike the rest of us.

Just maybe don't ask her to babysit.

Side note – if you too have an audacious child like ours, for God's sake please don't get them a balance bike.

Another side note – we saw our friends in A&E with their little boy who had got a popcorn kernel stuck up his nose.

I think we made them feel better, to be honest.

Mate, this is absolutely the kind of stupid attempt at time-saving that I find myself doing all the time. I honestly thought it was a brilliant idea until the steam! I hadn't considered the steam. I was reading this thinking, 'I bet she held the iron on her kid too long, rookie mistake.' I have now made a mental note to never iron an item of clothing while my child is wearing it . . . without turning the steam off and making sure there is no water in the iron. Thanks for the advice!

Please promise me you'll never actually do this.

I do mad shit like that all the time. I broke my laptop in a flat I lived in because I dropped it from the mezzanine balcony in the bedroom down on to the sofa because I was carrying too much stuff. I relate to your mam in this instance a LOT more than I should! Which is worrying.

Extremely.

I honestly still find it hard thinking about when Robin lost his teeth. It was absolutely horrific. All jokes aside, fair play to Rosie, she was cool, calm and collected throughout, and I was an absolute mess. I genuinely almost fainted like a damsel in distress in an old movie. I'm no help at all in those kind of situations, I just panic and go to the worst possible scenario in my head. If I'd been on my own with him we'd still be there now, both just crying and snotting on each other.

I still remember the first time he ever hurt himself . . . It stays with you . . .

When Robin was about four months old I was downstairs and Rosie was upstairs in the bathroom with him. He was sitting in his little seat on the tile floor while she got ready. She went to pick him up by picking up the entire seat; we both know now that you should NEVER DO THIS with these seats. They are not meant to be carried – the weight distribution is weird – and it spun backwards flipping Robin out and on to the bathroom tiles – head first. I heard the bang from downstairs, I can hear it now as I type this. I heard Rosie shout and Robin begin to cry. She ran downstairs with him and we started to get him ready to take him to hospital. There was a large bump on his head and he was crying uncontrollably. We got him ready and started out the door for the hospital, but in possibly one of the most common parenting moments, we started to think that maybe he didn't need to go to hospital. His crying had stopped a bit. Google said that as long as he's not going to sleep or becoming drowsy, a head bump is OK, and a quick call to the all-knowing oracle mother-in-law Sandra brought back the same advice. We went back into the house, Robin crying, Rosie crying, me crying . . . That was the first time we experienced those feelings. The rollercoaster of emotions that comes from this all-encompassing love you have for your little creation: the fear that they might be seriously hurt, the panic as you frantically try to fix the problem, the guilt that Rosie felt, and for me, the main emotion . . . the absolute pure euphoric relief that it wasn't me who dropped him! Better than sex!

OAP Sesh

I'm having a bit of a mare. I'm currently saving to buy my own house so I'm living with my parents. At 28 you can imagine the pain I go through every time I hear them 'at it'.

Thankfully I have managed to drown this out with your podcast.

Anyway, on to the other problem – do you have any advice on how I can approach my dad and tell him to stop leaving pubes on the bath? I'm going to do my nut soon, so please help!

Kim

Kim has kindly attached pictures of her dad's pubes on the bath with this email but thankfully our editors said no to printing them in the book, saving you all from the horror of it. Not me, unfortunately, as I was the one who opened the email. They were very long and very curly.

I'm so glad I don't read the emails.

You have no idea, babe.

This is a tricky one. You see, on the one hand I can totally see where you're coming from. Hearing your parents bucking (for non-podcast listeners, 'bucking' is a really classy way of describing sex. *Verb – To buck/Get one's buck on, etc.*), well, it's downright scary at any age, but to hear it at 28 must be utterly horrific!

On the other hand, though, I'm so buzzing for your mam and dad! How amazing that after all these years being married they still find each other attractive enough to have sex! Go on, them! Honestly, I'm beaming over here.

Chris and I are currently six years into our marriage and some nights I would rather rip his stupid face off than have sexual intercourse with him. This genuinely gives me so much hope! We too might still be bucking well into our twenty-eighth year of marriage!

This is probably not the response you were after, but as a child from a broken home #PrayForMe I'd give anything to hear my parents shacking up in the room next door to me.

Hang on.

Sorry, no, I absolutely would not.

You're bang on. I'm sorry, as soon as I've put myself in your situation I've realized and it has made me feel a little bit ill, to be honest. Bless you! Having to hear this on the regs! How selfish of them! They've had years of sex for God's sake! Give it a rest, guys!

Have you ever thought that all their loud late-night liaisons could be their sick way of trying to get rid of you faster?

Your dad – 'Howay, Moira, let's do it extra loud tonight! Might spur her on to buy her own bloody house!!!'

Your mam – 'Grab the bed, George! Harder!! Her bedroom

gets the best sun! It'd be a great little reading room! I SAID
HARDER!!!'

Just a thought.

I fear that the pubes in the bath situation is unfortunately
just your dad rightfully living his best life in his own house, a
house that he has no doubt worked most of his life to pay for.
So you can't really blame him for that, can you?

Maybe for your own sanity just try mentioning that you'd
love it if he could try not to leave his pubic hair lying about
everywhere. Or failing that you could buy him a trimmer for
Christmas. Maybe a box of hair removal cream? Worth a shot.

The newly trimmed penis would be a lovely inviting gift for your
mother too . . .

This part of your question reminds me of when I was younger
and my dad would constantly run to the bathroom naked in
the morning.

'Not so bad,' I hear you thinking? 'I do that all the time!'
Yes, but my siblings and I at the time were very much teen-
agers; the mere glimpse of a parent's private flesh would turn
our stomachs.

It unfortunately became such a frequent occurrence that
we took to verbally abusing him whenever we caught him
doing his nudist morning sprint across the landing. It led to
such turmoil in our house that my mam had to get involved.

As you can imagine, the family meeting surrounding this
subject got a bit heated, with my dad claiming that 'It's my
bloody house and I should be able to run to the bathroom

naked if I want.' And my mam countering, 'They're not little kids any more and they have their friends over now. How would they feel if they saw your bits?'

It actually happened once – my poor little mate is still probably rocking at the side of her bed reliving it now. Thanks, Dad.

After a lot of discussion and my dad still claiming that it's an outrage, we all came to a compromise. The next day my mam bought my dad a little towel that he could use to cover his private parts on his daily run to the bathroom. Unfortunately for us, this towel wasn't actually big enough to cover his backside, so we would still often see his arse running to the bathroom, just in time for breakfast.

Like I said. Compromise.

Rosie, your dad's love of being naked when you were a kid is possibly one of my favourite things ever. We talked on the podcast about how he was literally flabbergasted when you all asked him to start putting a top on when he was watching the TV, and now, to hear that he felt just as victimized when you put a stop to his morning naked sprints to the loo is amazing. And it makes sense, because I've actually had to pop to your dad's house a few times to drop stuff off or pick it up and he always answers the door in his boxer shorts . . . that man is a naturist!

My mam and dad stopped being naked in front of me at a young age, thank God! But I do remember that I had to get up for school when I was a teenager and go through their bedroom to get a shower in their en suite, attempting to hide my morning glory. That was awful. THEN my dad used to come and have his disgusting morning Dad piss in the toilet right next to the shower and it honestly smelt like he hadn't had a drink of water for a year. Absolutely horrific.

Kim, I've got to say I too am glad your parents are still smashing each other at this stage in their lives – well done, them! And by the sounds of things, they MUST even slightly hear mine and Rosie's voices while they do it . . . if you use the podcast to cover up the sound.

Maybe we should release a special episode which is just for their hammering sessions? We could play a sexy version of the jingle, shout words of encouragement and helpful tips like, 'Careful, George, remember your bad back . . . don't get carried away again!' Let us know, yeah?

Annoyed

The Seven-Year Itch . . .

I've heard people talk about 'the seven-year itch' for as long as I can remember.

Even as a child it was a well-known phrase. Obviously then I just thought people had itches for a really long time and when adults winked at each other or laughed about it I assumed the itch was located somewhere funny like their bum or something.

Turns out I was completely wrong. This imaginary itch is something that apparently happens seven years into a marriage. It's also a film (I think).

Chris and I are currently at year six and it's only now that I can 100 per cent resonate with this phrase. I am obviously extremely happily married, as I hope Chris is too . . . Chris?

It has its moments.

But honestly? It's bloody hard work, isn't it? Even after only six years the pressure of keeping a marriage together and happy and as exciting and passionate as the day it started is very intense and not always possible.

I don't know whether it's because you have a contractual bond to the other person that it feels so much more definite. A bit like a job, perhaps? A really testing full-time job, with someone who you occasionally/rarely have sex with and often bring up children together with.

They see parts of your life that you'd rather they didn't, but it's completely unavoidable as you live in the same house together 24/7.

Most of them would be easily avoidable if you just closed the bathroom door.

I remember the first time Chris happened to walk in on me shaving my vagina. Now I know what you're thinking – that's not that horrific. But you know when you would just rather they hadn't seen it? The positioning alone that you have to get yourself into is awful and it's just not a good look. I wanted him to think I was perfectly trimmed down there and that at any given moment of the day it would always be just like that, perfect!

I'm pretty sure I had one of my legs up on the bath too, you know – getting right in there, I was.

Mind, I suppose looking back, the vaginal shaving wasn't anywhere near as bad as the time I left the door wide open and he witnessed me taking a tampon out. Bless his heart, I thought he was going to faint!

I still have the nightmares.

I often wonder how some couples manage to keep things like this from each other. Why are Chris and I so unable to keep things private? I know on my part that it's sheer laziness. I hate closing the bathroom door after me.

SEE!

We only recently got a lock as guests were uncomfortable going for a wee in an unlockable toilet. But people can keep parts of their daily routine from their loved one for years. Take my mother-in-law, for example – she has never ever in over forty years of marriage passed wind in front of my father-in-law. Imagine that? Her poor bowels must be in agony! Chris only told me this a couple of years ago and I couldn't believe it.

They have however been extremely happily married for those forty years so maybe that's the secret to a healthy marriage? Keep your trumps in? I think I'd die. Honestly, I think it would kill me.

Rosie Ramsey buried here. Died from holding in her farts.

Judging by how much you fart these days, it would take about forty-five minutes of holding them in to kill you.

When Chris and I were relatively new to our relationship we went on holiday to Dubai. Chris was pulling out all the stops to impress me and I was lapping it up. I couldn't believe my luck, to be honest. He paid for the lot!

It was one of the most incredible holidays I've ever had – loads of new-relationship sex, tons of alcohol and seven full days of lying in the baking hot sun. Amazing.

What wasn't so amazing though was the fact that I had to hold in every single fart! Also the toilet in our hotel room had a GLASS door! A glass door, man?! Who designed this bloody hotel? You could see everything!

I didn't have a shite for almost four days. It was agony.

Luckily it wasn't just me, Chris was also in a lot of pain. It would appear that he was also stopping himself from passing wind, and equally terrified to empty his bowels directly behind a glass door that his new girlfriend was sat mere metres away from.

It was on this very holiday that we were forced to have the 'fart conversation'.

Rosie – 'So, I'm not sure how to say this but you might have noticed that I eat quite a lot of vegetables? Yeah, I really like them. Only problem is they can often make me a bit gassy. Yeah, I'm actually quite a gassy person, to be honest. I've been trying to hold them all in while we've been away and to be honest with you, Chris, I'm in a bad way.'

Chris – 'Oh my God, Rosie! So am I! I'm in bits over here! I'm a broken man!'

Rosie – 'Can we?'

Chris – 'Shall we?'

Rosie and Chris holding hands and looking deeply into one another's eyes – 'Let's fart in front of each other from now on! I love you.'

I honestly can't tell you all how much this genuinely changed my life. I had never farted in front of a girlfriend regularly before and I had spent so many nights in AGONY after meals in the house. I honestly thought I had some kind of medical problem . . . until Rosie said, 'Did you never fart in front of your ex?' and I replied, 'No, never', to which Rosie responded, 'Were you not just in pain all the time?' – then the penny dropped. Yes, I was. I would eat a spag bol and spend the rest of the night in the foetal position watching *The Wire* and fighting back tears.

I know this is a book and you have no way of responding, but have you had the fart chat? If not, do you want to? Here's hoping this might spur you on! It can't be a healthy way to live.

DO IT! *The Wire* is so much easier to follow when you're not writhing in agony.

I often wonder if Chris and I had never got married whether we'd be feeling this itch.

Would we be happier not married? Safe in the knowledge that we could potentially up and leave at any given moment?

There'd be no lawyer's fees, you'd just take what was yours and go. Nobody would be horrifically shocked by the news of your separation as they would be about you ending your marriage. Hmmm, I wonder.

Well, we went a bit further though, didn't we?

Marriage.

Child.

Co-hosting a podcast.

Co-authoring a book.

The paperwork involved in our potential divorce would be intimidating.

I'd rather just be miserable for the rest of my life. But you'd be miserable too, and that would at least make me a little bit happy.

I know a few people who never want to get married. I understand that more than you might realize. You see, marriage per se was never hugely on my agenda. I just wanted to meet someone and be really happy.

I didn't dream about my wedding day, I never dressed up as a bride when I was a kid. I didn't have a mood board on Pinterest. (Until I was engaged, that is, then a switch just flicked on. Come on, everybody does!)

The one and only reason I got married was because I was (sorry, erm, am?) so madly, head over heels in love with Chris that I just wanted to celebrate it! I wanted to shout it from the rooftops! I'M IN LOVE! SOMEBODY ACTUALLY LOVES ME!! I was more surprised than anybody about it, to be honest. Especially after the whole tampon fiasco . . .

Chris proposed after only six months of us being together. It was so quick and I really wasn't expecting it. If somebody were to ask me if they should get engaged after just six months of being together I'd probably laugh in their face. Who does this? Surely that's far too soon? You don't even know each other! Have you even had the fart chat??!?!

The fart chat was the moment I knew you were the one . . .

Well, here comes the hypocrite . . . because I said yes!

I couldn't believe that someone could love/like me so much that they would ask me to spend their whole life with them.

Out of all the people in the world, this person has chosen to spend the rest of their life with me! He's not a dick, he makes you cups of juice without you asking, he gets on with your friends, you're yet to have a proper argument, he's a happy drunk AND he is absolutely lush! He's chosen me! Little old fanny-shaving me! Best. Feeling. Ever.

Oh, that's made me dead happy!

It really is a wonderful feeling. It all felt so unbelievably romantic! I mean, the proposal was pretty shite, to be fair . . . but the fact that he was doing it was amazing. If you know what I mean?

And the happiness has gone.

The proposal . . .

Chris and I had been together officially for six months.

I had moved myself into his bungalow – yes, we moved ridiculously fast and also yes, Chris's first house was a bunga-low. Bachelor bungalow if you will.

'The One-Storey Glory'.

Not that he got much of a chance at that lifestyle, bless him. I had my bags well and truly unpacked after three months of moving in! I promise you, it wasn't intentional! We just genuinely really clicked. And I may or may not have been living with my mam at the time. And because we are basically the same person we fought like cat and dog. She was happy to see the back of me.

I think it also helped that we had known each other for a large portion of our lives.

I knew he wasn't a massive wrong 'un and he had a good job, etc. I thought, Rosie, you could do much worse, babes.

What a review.

The bungalow was a brand spanking new-build on an eerily quiet cul-de-sac a stone's throw away from the South Shields coastline.

The gentleman who lived opposite us used to hoover his driveway twice a week. Very odd to watch and I still to this day don't know how his hoover didn't pack in.

If Chris and I went out on an evening, when we returned the neighbours would be twitching the curtains. It was that sort of street. Lovely folks, don't get me wrong, but we were by far the youngest people on the street by about 35 years.

We had two blissful years there. Like, honestly, pure utter bliss. No cross words, loads of sleep, parties. This is the house we went back to the day after our wedding, and I have very happy memories of that place, even if the gravel-hoovering neighbour was a tad odd.

Anyway, the proposal, sorry.

Chris was away working in Montreal at a comedy festival. It was the first time in our six months together that we'd been apart for an extended amount of time.

Chris worked away a lot as he still does now, but he always comes home at least three nights a week. I missed him so much that week, like a disgusting amount. Chris felt the same way. Obviously, we chatted on the phone, but it's never the same.

Unbeknownst to me, at Heathrow Airport Chris was sat outside a well-known jewellery shop. He was probably hungover and most definitely suffering from jet lag. He decided (very spur of the moment, if I may say) to purchase an engagement ring. Pour moi! Now that I know him better this doesn't surprise me any more. Chris is extremely impulsive when it comes to buying stuff. He's like a little magpie – if it's shiny and new he'll buy it.

Over the years he's bought so much shite I swear local retailers see him walk in and rub their hands together.

In one day he once bought an outdoor swimming/paddling pool, a six-by-six-foot trampoline, a bike AND a remote control helicopter. He invited his mate Carl round and it was a really sorry sight, I tell you. This was all before we had our son, so it wasn't like he bought it all for him! ANYWAY. I digress. Back to the proposal . . .

When Chris returned home later that day he was knackered from a long flight and a hard week's work. It was about 9 p.m. and we were both sat watching telly.

Chris had been asleep on my lap for about an hour and a half. I'd stayed so still in order not to wake him that my foot had gone to sleep in the process. But if you remember, this was only six months in, very much the pleasing each other stage, so I ignored my dying foot and watched him sleep. Yes, we were head over heels in love at this point so I would sometimes watch him sleep. Please don't judge me. I don't do it any more, I swear!

You blatantly do, creep.

When Chris woke up from his nap he asked if I wouldn't mind getting him a cup of tea from the kitchen. I said of course not but found it odd as it was rather late for tea since he doesn't usually have any sort of caffeine after 6 p.m.

I'm 84 years old.

I ignored those thoughts and hobbled to the kitchen to get a cup of tea. While I was there Chris yelled to me to take my time. Take my time? Why ever for? What's he got planned? Oh God, I'm going to go back in there and he's going to be dressed in a Mankini or something, isn't he? This was also back when we used to have really regular sex, so another thought was that he will be starkers giving me the eye! He doesn't even want this tea, does he? The little trickster!! Right, Rosie, he's been away a whole week, this is exciting, isn't it? Check your bits, babe. You're all good, glad you had that bath now. Have a quick Tic Tac out the shit drawer and you're set!

Chris about ten minutes later – 'OK, you can come in now!!!'

What the hell is he doing?

What happened next I'll never forget for as long as I live . . .

I walked into our living room, in our little bungalow . . .

Erm, one-storey glory.

There were candles lit all around the room (aaaaah, that's what took him so long!), Bruno Mars's 'Marry You' was playing from one of Chris's spur-of-the-moment-purchase Bose speakers and there he was, at the entrance of the room, down on one knee.

He was crying! Then I was crying! Is this really happening?

He didn't say anything for ages. I said, 'What's going on?' To which he held out a little blue gift bag tied with a ribbon . . .

The bloody div left the ring box in the bag, didn't he? So instead of proposing by opening a ring box to expose a ring, you know like sane people do, my fiancé-to-be got down on one knee, started to cry and handed me a gift bag.

I WAS JET-LAGGED!!

As you can imagine, I was a little perplexed.

'No really, what's happening, Chris? Do you want this tea?'

'OH SHIT! I didn't take it out the bag! Fuck! Ah sorry, Rosie!'

Finally takes ring box out of said bag . . .

'Rosie Winter, will you marry me?'

Oh my God! He's asking me to marry him! Holy shit!!! Hahahahahha! This is what it feels like! OK, well, answer him!

'Are you sure? You've only just woke up!'

As if I had just found the ring under the fucking sofa!

And that was it. Our proposal. Just the two of us in the living room of our first home, in our pyjamas.

It was perfect.

Oh, I said yes. But I'm guessing you probably already know that.

What Rosie has left out of that story is that she also said, through tears, 'Why have you proposed to me while I'm wearing my old PE shorts?', but anyway . . .

I had absolutely no idea what the 'seven-year itch' was until I was told Rosie was writing a chapter about it. I'm assuming that the main cause of the 'itch' is thinking that maybe there is something better out there, or that you want to be free and single and ready to mingle again. NO THANKS. I can honestly say, I don't think it's something I'll be feeling anytime soon. Mainly because I literally could not be arsed to go back out into the world of dating. Ever. I'd rather die alone.

Every time we do the podcast we get questions and stories from people who are currently trawling the dating pool trying to find their future partner and it gives me a bit of a panic attack imagining myself in their position. I know some people enjoy being single, I'm just saying . . . it's not for me. If a marriage is a full-time job, then dating is just like one massive long job interview with the dangling possibility of sex at the end of it.

I've not had many TERRIBLE dates in my time, no real disasters or anything, but I've had some where the conversation was absolutely non-existent. I mean, cringeworthy, zero banter, sitting in silence nights. On one occasion I got a text after one of these Nando's silences claiming that she'd had a 'great night' and wanted to 'do it again some time' – are you fucking serious? Can't you just sit in your house and not talk to anyone? Do you have to drag me into it? No offence, but if that's your idea of a 'great night' – silently watching me inhale a chicken wrap – then our possible future life together would be a bit one-sided . . . I can inhale a wrap without an audience.

I honestly love being married. It's amazing being part of a team. Knowing that someone is there for you emotionally and also legally obliged to be . . . they make promises to God and everything, it's pretty water-tight! And I personally think being married makes you able to get away with a little bit more arse-holery than you could in a non-marital relationship. You can get away with a lot more when splitting up involves more paper-work and financial issues than actual emotions.

Sometimes I might say or do something and the idea that Rosie will want to divorce me for it pops into my head, but then it's quickly shooed away by the immediate thought of 'Ah, she couldn't be arsed to go through all that shit!' So I continue to berate her on her horrific dishwasher stacking skills (or lack of).

An Ode to Sleep

Me and my girlfriend both have a couple's bedtime (i.e., go to bed at the same time). One of us has to be up at 4:30 a.m. due to shift work and the other is off work, but we will both still go to bed at the same time.

I have spoken to different couples and they all seem to have different bedtimes. So one will go to bed and the other will stay up and watch TV.

Do you go to bed at the same time, or does one stay up and watch TV and come to bed later on??

Cory and Leanne

I imagine as you read this, you're sitting side by side under the blankets at 8 p.m. . . . . You maniacs!

I've got to side with the couples you have spoken to and agree that you are very strange (yes, I know they didn't say this to you, but trust me, they said it as soon as you left).

Myself and Rosie will go to bed at the same time 99 per cent of the time, but that's because I work away so much and when I am at home we are normally getting up at the same time with Robin. If I ever had to be up at 4:30 a.m. the next day and attempted to drag Rosie away from *Real Housewives of Shoutsville County* to come to bed with me at 8 p.m., there would be absolute hell on!

This is true.

I get shouted at if I dare suggest we go to bed before 10 p.m. these days as it is.

This is also true.

I'm not totally hating on you both here, I think it's quite sweet that you feel the need to be around each other that much, but do you not have anything to watch on your own? Nothing on Netflix that only one of you fancies? And if one of you can't get to sleep, do they just sit and stare at the other one like a killer? I'm going to go ahead and assume that you haven't been together that long and guess that this will pass . . .

Oh, it passes all right.

Sleep becomes a real bone of contention when you have kids. Your entire attitude towards it changes. Don't get me wrong, I still absolutely LOVE it, I just don't have the same relationship with it now. I can't think of the word 'sleep' without thinking of the sentence 'Why the fuck won't he go to sleep?!'

I honestly can't remember the last time I woke up and wasn't absolutely knackered.

Maybe when I was about 27? I sometimes wake up feeling like I haven't even been asleep. And when there is a 4-year-old shouting you out of bed, it really doesn't help matters.

To be fair, Rosie has done the majority of getting up with Robin his entire life, as I've been away so much, and I really don't know how she's coped.

I haven't, Chris. I'm a walking fucking zombie most days.

One of the most annoying things on earth is when a child wakes up crazy early, demands to go downstairs and start the day, then acts like a full-on dickhead all morning because they are tired. It's torture. You want to scream, 'WE COULD HAVE STILL BEEN IN BED, YOU IDIOT!'

He's going to be absolutely gutted when he's 18, hung-over and me and Rosie are blasting music and dancing on his bed. I can't wait.

The greatest sentence in the world for me has become 'I'll get up with him tomorrow morning.' When Rosie says it, I could honestly weep with joy, and I know it's the same for her when I say it.

A lie-in is the currency most marriages run on. You can get a lot for a lie-in. You can get a night out with your mates, you can justify a rather expensive luxury purchase or, Rosie's favourite, you can use it to control the evening's TV viewing.

'Come on, let's watch an episode of George Clarke . . . I'll get up with Robin in the morning.'

Fuck, yes! Get George on right now! Get him on and get a bottle of beer in my hand. I'm going to chug every time he says 'amazing space'.

In the early stages of having a child most married couples play a daily game of tiredness Top Trumps with each other. This is where you both attempt to one-up each other on who is the most tired by listing recent times you were up in the night, up early in the morning or the things that you have done during that day which you believe amount to more energy exerted than your partner. Rosie and me used to play this while both face down in bed, while Robin shouted to get our attention over the baby monitor from his cot. (God, I miss the days when he couldn't physically come and jump on your sleeping body!)

Ah God, me too.

Robin shouting, we both wake up.

   'You get him, love, I was up with him yesterday.'

   'Oh, but you went to bed earlier than me.'

   'Yeah, but I've had a terrible sleep, I tossed and turned all night.'

   'But I've got work tonight!'

   'Right, well, you get up with him now, and I'll come down at eight and you can come back to bed.'

   'OK.'

We used to do this quite a lot, actually. I would get up at about 5:30 a.m.... sometimes before CBeebies had even begun to broadcast – the horror of it! Rosie would then sleep until 8 a.m., then she would come downstairs and tag me out, and I'd head back up to bed to sleep.

The lie-in is a precious gift in our house. And when you've received a lie-in, you better not come downstairs once you have woken up and claim to be tired or even dare to yawn in the presence of the other or there will be HELL ON, MATE!

Nothing worse than being up all morning watching *Bing* and knocking up one of the ever-changing breakfasts your toddler invents while trying to squeeze in a coffee and a cheeky look at your socials only to be greeted two hours later by a foot-dragging, pyjama-wearing, arse-scratching yawner who rolls down from the promised land claiming to be somehow 'still tired' or uttering the worst words imaginable: 'I think I've overslept.'

You are literally describing yourself – you do realize this, right? Also just want to add here if I may, you have NEVER woken up and not told me that you've had a terrible night's sleep. Never.

Carry on . . .

I want to take a moment to relay a quick message to everyone who doesn't have kids . . .

Can you remember when you were a child? And you were in a mood, or crying or having a little tantrum? And your parents would say, 'Oh no, I think you're tired', and you would scream the house down claiming not to be tired. I've got some news for you . . . YOU WERE FUCKING TIRED!

You were so fucking tired, and that my friend is why you were acting like a complete and utter dick. Call your parents right this second and apologize.

How much MORE do you love your kids when they sleep in? Seriously, my adoration of my son is always at a minimum of 100 per cent, no matter what happens, no matter what he's doing. He could be washing my new car with a brick and I'd still love every ounce of him . . . But if me and Rosie are woken up by her alarm and not him shouting and screaming, and given a chance to gather our thoughts before going straight into parenting mode for the day . . . that bad boy goes up to 150 per cent.

You're bang on there, Ramsey.

I absolutely HATE being tired. It kills me. Honestly, I'd happily do a deal with the devil so that I never have to sleep ever again (bear with me) if I could function fully on zero hours' sleep and never have any adverse health effects or some kind of break-down. Imagine feeling fresh as a daisy all the time, I'd be over the moon! I'd live my life as usual during the day, then on a night, I would play on my PlayStation or watch stuff on TV that Rosie doesn't like. It would be amazing. I'd complete Netflix and Amazon Prime in a month.

The fact that we haven't evolved to survive without sleep by now is an absolute travesty. Does no one else think it's weird that we all lie down and stay still for almost half the day with our eyes shut and then SUDDENLY it's morning?! It's nuts. I'd sack it off in a heartbeat if I could. But as it is, I need my sleep and if I don't get my desired hours, I've been known to burst into tears on a delayed train to London.

At about 3 p.m. every day I hit a wall that feels like someone has just spiked my afternoon tea with sleeping pills. If I'm sitting down at the time, you're not getting me out of that chair, even if you set the house on fire. I'd just sit there and cook. No idea how it happens. I've tried more caffeine, I've tried less caffeine, I've tried going to the gym, going on walks – nothing works. I think I'm designed to nap in the afternoons, but I fear for my safety if I declared to Rosie that every afternoon when I'm home 3–4 is sleepy times and I am under no circumstances to be disturbed. I think I'd be woken up by the sound of my belongings being thrown on to the drive.

Don't even think about it.

I say all this, but I've worked away for a lot of Robin's life, so I have missed a good chunk of the bedtime trauma and the mind-numbing mornings . . . I am told this a lot by Rosie, who claims to still be shell-shocked by it all. I will happily admit now that I would not have coped. At all. Would I, love?

Absolutely fucking not.

During Robin's first year Chris worked away from home for approximately 200 nights. He would call me most mornings at 11 a.m. saying he'd just woken up. I often used to cry down the phone or not long after.

- Chris could have 72 hours of sleep and still complain that he hadn't slept well.
- If Robin can't sleep and comes downstairs crying, Chris has a small panic attack.
- If Chris did have a little nap at 3–4 p.m., he would wake up cranky, complain he felt ill, then come bedtime he'd be wide awake and whinge on again

that he felt ill and exclaim, 'Why can't I get to sleep?'
So no, I don't think an afternoon nap is appropriate
for this stage in your life, babe.

We are currently trying for another baby. Chris has booked
a tour in. Coincidence? You decide.

Slob Wife, Slob Life

They say opposites attract and I think I can speak for myself and Rosie when I say, we have no idea whether that is true or not. We couldn't possibly tell, as sometimes we are the exact same person in so many ways and other times we are so different it's actually mind-boggling that we can live under the same roof.

I am a clean freak, or maybe more accurately a 'tidy' freak. I just hate it when stuff is not in its right place . . . or at least a place that looks right. I can't bear it. I literally can't relax if something is cluttering up the room I'm in. When I got my first flat on my own (a duplex apartment in Manchester – sounds posh, but it wasn't. Imagine the reception area of a big office building but with a bed and a TV in it. Soulless, cold, awful), I would sometimes waste entire nights 'pottering about' but not actually doing anything. I'd stick the TV on, sit on the sofa then spend the whole night getting up to tidy shit, or hoover a bit of dust I saw, or straighten a pile of DVDs. Pointless.

I kind of do the same now. If Rosie goes out for the night and I'm left at home, I'll rarely watch anything on TV. Firstly, there is absolutely nothing of mine recorded on the Sky Box. It's half cluttered up with *Mr Men* and *Blaze and the Monster Machines* for Robin, and Rosie has the rest of the hard drive space filled with every conceivable incarnation of televised buying, selling, letting homes or fixing up dilapidated French shithole castles.

You best not be slagging off *Escape to the Chateau*, Ramsey!

The latter is the most annoying because not only is the Sky Box full of them but every few days she'll watch an episode that she particularly enjoys and I have to spend forty-five minutes talking her out of the idea of buying one and moving our entire family to France to run a fucking B&B.

ONE DAY I'LL HAVE MY DREAM CHATEAU! *BONJOUR!*

Anyway, if I want to sit and watch TV, the room I'm in has to be tidy or I can't relax. Rosie on the other hand could sit and watch some prick ridding their original wooden chateau front door of woodworm as the house literally burns down around her. She will happily watch fifteen straight episodes of *The Good Wife* with a sink full of dishes and a hoover in the middle of the room while sitting on a pile of dirty washing. And I am a bit jealous of that.

I feel you're exaggerating a tad here, Chris. I wouldn't have brought the hoover in unless it was absolutely necessary, let's be honest.

I am worse when I'm on my own. When I'm with Rosie she just tells me not to worry about the mess and I can put it to the back of my mind. But we usually end up having an argument at the end of the night about whether to go straight to bed or stick everything in the dishwasher before we go up. Literally. Every.

Night. If I get up in the morning and I'm greeted by a pile of washing and a dishwasher full of dirty dishes I am actually devastated and I'll sort them all out before I have my morning coffee.

I just want to clarify here that Chris's idea of mess is not a usual person's idea of mess. When he talks about leftover dishes in the sink, he means like three plates and perhaps a spoon. This is ridiculous, to be honest. The way you're describing this, Chris, you'd think we lived in a flipping hostel!

She's not a disgusting animal.

Christ alive! Chris!

She's very clean, never smells bad, she's just messy . . . Fucking hell, that sounds like I'm reviewing a dog. She will just do things in her own sweet time, and if I DARE to enquire as to how long she's planning to put off a certain job . . . you can bet she's going to double that time in her head, just because I asked.

Yep.

Here are some of her greatest hits:

OK. Wow, so this is a whole chapter just slagging me off, isn't it? Brilliant. Howay then, let's hear it.

The Dishwasher

She cannot and will never know how to stack a dishwasher. It's just never going to happen. I've given up on the entire thing. In the early days, before I'd given up all hope, I used to get myself angry about it. I'd open the dishwasher and it would look like an earthquake had hit a crockery cupboard (still does to this day) and I would be stupid enough to shout over to her and tell her it was a disgrace. I'd say things like:

'Rosie, these plates are touching each other, the water won't get in to clean them!'

'This pan is far too big, the spinner won't spin.'

'Why is there a shoe in here!?'

Right, well that's an outright lie.

I'd often ask her to come and stand while I quickly showed her what she had done wrong.

(Now yes, there will be people reading this thinking, 'What a prick this bloke is' – and you are exactly the same as Rosie, and do you know what? We wouldn't get on. Thankfully I love and adore my wife, so this is just something I put up with. You . . . the person thinking this right now? You can fuck off. You're a slob, mate.)

This attempted dishwasher-stacking crash course would always end in a fight. Or even worse, she would just stand there with a glazed look on her face taking absolutely none of it in. I might as well have been telling the dishwasher how to stack itself.

If only, eh?

So now, I just have to restack the mess on my own, but here's the kicker, this is what really drives me mad ... If she sees me fixing her mess, SHE GETS ANNOYED! Incredibly, she would rather I just left it and we half-filled a dishwasher then when it's finished, remove the STILL FUCKING FILTHY dishes and wash them in the sink or put it back on in some kind of endless cycle of never learning from our dishwasher mistakes.

'Oh, this pasta bowl is still dirty.'
BACK ON
'Oh, this pasta bowl is still dirty.'
BACK ON
– repeat until you die –

Probably a better way of life than the fascist dishwasher regime I'm currently living under.

Recycling

Oh. Great. There's more.

Rosie Ramsey has absolutely no idea what is a recyclable material and what is not.

She is pretty sure you can recycle paper and cardboard but has absolutely no clue of the difference between the two.

One is soft, one is brown. Right?

SO the paper is often in the cardboard bit and vice versa.

She knows you can recycle plastic trays, for example, from a packet of prawns, but she is 50/50 on whether you can recycle the peelable plastic so she just leaves it on every time anyway. EVERY. SINGLE. TIME. And when I say, 'Rosie, you can't recycle this bit', she always, ALWAYS replies, 'Oh sorry, I can never remember if you can or not.' Rosie, I love you, but oh my God it's been six years, you have prawns literally once a week, sometimes twice. TRY AND REMEMBER!

Funny your memory isn't too shabby when there's a release date of the new series of 'Housewives Argue the Colour of Shite' to remember.

I have to personally trawl through the recycling containers before taking them to the big bin or the bin men would blacklist us from their route. The shit I've found in there: plastic bags, bubble wrap, broken coat hangers, cotton buds (used), light bulbs . . . and if Sandra has been round and had a pop at it, fuck me, all bets are off.

Oh Chris, stop whingeing! You know you love it!

Clothes

Clothes? How can you slag me off re clothes? THEY'RE A NECESSITY!

Some women have a couple of wardrobes. Some have lots. Some have whole rooms filled with them. Rosie has one wardrobe.

One massive wardrobe. It's a walk-in wardrobe. You access it via our front door and the entire family sleeps in it. It's our entire fucking house.

BAHAHAHA! I honestly had no idea where you were going there.

The majority of stuff can be found on the bathroom floor. Dirty, clean – who knows? Some of it can be found on the shelf next to the sink in the upstairs bathroom, that's a new one she's been doing recently.

You said to stop putting it on the floor! So I've been putting stuff on the shelf! WHAT DO YOU WANT FROM ME???

A lot of it can be found on the floor RIGHT NEXT TO THE DIRTY-WASHING BASKET. When Rosie has a bath, the clothes she has climbed out of will remain on the bathroom floor until the next time she has a bath, at which point they will be removed and replaced by the clothes she removes for that bath.

It's called a system.

YET if a pair of shoes belonging to myself are left in the hallway for more than three minutes there is absolute hell on. The hypocrisy of the slob, ladies and gentlemen. 'Why is your tiny bit of clutter cluttering my fuck ton of clutter?!'

Firstly, a lot of this information is fabricated.

Secondly, I think they should label recyclable products better as it can be very confusing.

Thirdly, the hallway is sacred. It's people's first impression of our home, I like this area to be kept nice and tidy. Nobody sees our upstairs bathroom or the inside of our fucking dishwasher, so frankly I don't give a shit what's happening inside either of them. The hallway I do. The same goes for the front door. I was once told that if you have a dirty front door then you have a dirty vagina. This has stayed with me for years. I would hate for someone to think that I've got a dirty vagina, hence why it is always nipping clean.

My vagina is also spotless.

Now, there's a cupboard just next to the front door, it's aptly named the shoe cupboard. Want to hazard a guess as to why? IT'S WHERE THE SHOES LIVE! Put your shoes in there!

No matter how messy someone is, they will always have a certain thing that they get particular about:

My husband's a slob and I have hundreds of beefs, but his biggest beef with me is that I put my empty crisp packet/rubbish in my empty glass or mug when I'm finished with it. In my head it's tidier and easier to carry to the kitchen. He fecking hates it. What's your take on this?

Laura

I feel your pain here, Laura. You, like me, have had to relax all of your inner tidiness habits for fear of either living in an endless argument or losing your mind running around cleaning up after a lazy, messy prick. And yet, here, your fella has this one thing he has a go at you for.

But I have to agree with him. Rosie does that and it's fucking rank. Just put the rubbish next to the mug or glass.

'Easier to carry to the kitchen'? You're walking across your house, not clearing a restaurant at closing time. When you put the wrapper in there it gets the dregs of the liquid on it and you have to tip it into the bin like you work in a pub. It's unsettling and I can see where he's coming from.

Laura, oh my dear Laura, I feel your pain. You're simply multi-tasking by placing the said wrapper in a container so as to not forget it or drop it on the floor. Fact of the matter is we'll never win against the opinions of our other halves.

I suggest we meet up, look for some land and start a commune together where we can be free from this tyranny!

On the Road Again

Missing someone is a weird concept when you think about it. We have so much technology these days, you can literally see someone's face and talk to them, but still miss them because they're not physically there. Some people can cope with this brilliantly and use it to their advantage. When I did *Strictly Come Dancing*, Karen and her fella David used to FaceTime each other and watch Netflix together when she was in the hotel and he was at home, which I thought was so sweet, but at the same time, I could just see me and Rosie ending up arguing if we did that. We have enough trouble when we're in the same room watching something, to be fair. We pause stuff every five minutes to say something and I have to ask her to leave her phone in another room or she'll just subconsciously pick it up, start watching some pricks on TikTok and then get me to explain the MASSIVE plot point she just missed.

I thought you liked doing that?!?

We once tried to watch the same movie at the same time while sitting next to each other on a plane. Hers was a fraction of a second ahead of mine and I could see it out of the corner of my eye for the entire film. I couldn't take my eyes off it. It drove me mental. At one point in the movie, someone was aiming a gun at someone and I knew her screen was going to give me a split-second spoiler before mine caught up. If we even attempted a FaceTime Netflix and chill we wouldn't get past the opening credits.

I'd still like to try, as it sounds quite romantic and we're lacking that if I'm honest.

Then again, I'm coming at this from six years of marriage . . . In the early days we might have managed it. Not now, no way. We can't agree on what to watch when we've spent the day together, let alone if we're in different corners of the country in different moods. To be fair, her default viewing is *Real Housewives* or *Escape to the Chateau*.

I wish you'd stop slagging off *Housewives* and *Chateau*. It's really beginning to upset me.

And I can count on one hand the amount of times I've agreed to have either of those as our main evening's viewing. In fact, just the other day, Rosie was feeling a bit down and I said, 'You can put *Chateau* on if you want,' and she actually cried. Literally tears of joy were running down her face.

It's true. I couldn't believe my luck!

I felt like a right bastard. 'Look, if it means that much to you, I'll just go in the office and play on my PlayStation and you can watch it every night!' But she won't have that. I have to be in the room. We have to be spending quality time together, watching something that one of us doesn't enjoy. And that, my friends, is marital compromise!

I mean, God forbid we actually spend time together . . .

It's because I work away, to be fair. Working away does strange things to your relationship. Every TV show and film you watch depicts the man coming back home and the woman running into his arms. They scoop them up and kiss passionately and then have instant sex and everything is amazing again. That's bullshit. It's more like a longer version of those videos you see online of a stolen dog being reunited with its real owner after three years. There's a definite sniffing-out process when you walk back in the house. Yes, there's an initial hug and excitement, but then there's a period of 'OK, why has my stuff been moved?', 'What have you deleted from the Skybox?', 'Why have you moved the sofas around AGAIN?!'

We once had an argument on the way home from her picking me up from the train station. We had our beautiful *Love Actually* closing credits cuddles and kisses on the station platform, then got into the car and immediately pissed each other off. The bliss must have lasted three minutes, max.

If that, babe.

You get used to your own space and your partner gets used to you being away.

Hear, hear!

You miss them but then you get used to them not being there. It messes with your head. Sometimes I pine to get home then when I'm home I wish I was out on the road. It works the other way too . . . Rosie will say, 'You need to go back on tour because I have loads of new stuff recorded and ready to watch.' Brilliant. Thanks, loving wife!

They've put *Escape to the Chateau DIY* on once a day! I'm struggling to keep up! You're getting in the way of my French chateau-owning dreams, Chris!

Apparently I need to get myself back on the road because the makers of *Real Housewives* have found yet another area of America inhabited by a bunch of back-stabbing, shit-talking maniacs.

Oooooh, yeah, them too.

When we first had Robin I worked away A LOT. I went back on tour when Robin was ten days old. Shocking that, innit? In my defence, it was my DVD tour so I had to do it and record the show, but I genuinely remember telling audiences that I had a two-week-old baby and getting gasps of shock from them in a kind of 'Why the fuck are you here then?!' manner . . . But on the flip side of that, I DID get a very angry message from a lovely lady on Facebook for cancelling a gig in Sheffield the NIGHT ROSIE WENT INTO LABOUR because this apparently ruined her boyfriend's thirty-first birthday plans to come and see me. So who knows what people think?

Still can't believe you did that, like. Proper shocking.

Rosie was a stay-at-home mam for the first few years of Robin's life and we used to argue almost constantly about who had it worse. She always claimed it was her, I always claimed it was me. The grass is always greener, isn't it? I was knackered from performing and travelling non-stop, but she saw it as a jolly. And I saw what she was doing as just some lovely time off. You could argue that everyone's perception is different so no one would be right or wrong in this situation ... but I can tell you right now. It was her. She was right. The COVID-19 lockdown proved this beyond any doubt. Kids are just absolutely relentless.

THANK YOU!!! I didn't need your clarification, but it's nice to see you've finally recognized it.

We are currently, at the time of writing this, in week six of UK lockdown and working from home with our 4-year-old son. I've always talked about taking a big chunk of time off to spend at home with the family, it's something I've always wanted ... but not like this. NOT LIKE THIS!

From the moment he opens his eyes in the morning until the moment he closes them at night he is an energy-filled, noisy, non-stop machine. I can't get a minute's peace. I go on my government-allowed bike ride once a day just for some alone time. I sometimes get back and just sit in the garden on my own for a moment to get my breath back, because the second I walk in the door I know it'll be:

'Daddy, can we play Police?'

'Daddy, can we take all the cushions off the sofa and jump over them?'

'Daddy, can we just do anything that stops you from sitting still or having any kind of chill time at all?'

It's often said that kids 'keep you on your toes'. For me, this isn't entirely accurate as it implies that they're always in some kind of danger so you have to be ready to pounce. A better explanation that I can offer is that kids are like that manager at work who always wants you to look busy. Know what I mean? When I worked in All:Sports one of the managers I had used to just find shit for you to do if there were no customers or, heaven forbid, if we had finished all the jobs we had to do for the day. I once had to go into the stockroom and count the spare coat hangers, just because it was a sunny Sunday afternoon and no one was coming into the shop. The same bloke would come over if you were just standing there and say, 'Do something or I'll find you something to do' – that's EXACTLY what Robin is like. If he sees me sitting down or taking a break, he'll find me something to do. Sometimes the little shit starts the sentence asking me for something before the idea of what he wants me to do has actually formed in his head:

Me sitting having a cup of tea

'Daddy . . .'

'Yes, son?'

'What are you doing?'

'Just having a cup of tea, son.'

'Well, well . . . can you, could you, I need you to . . . can you find me a . . . where's my . . . can you build me a new police plane out of Lego?'

I swear, that's a direct quote! Feeling his way along that demand in the dark, he was! Clutching at straws! He *has* a police plane! I have rebuilt it a million times. The other day he honestly made me take apart the police plane to make a slightly different police plane. Sometimes he'll hand me a single, flat, one-brick-by-one-brick piece of blue Lego – you know the bit, it's about the size of a crumb? He'll hand me it and say, 'Here, Daddy, can you build a Batman with that?' – what is this, *Taskmaster*?! The day he asks me to count coat hangers I'll probably do it for a moment's quiet. When the lockdown is lifted I'll be dropping him off at my parents' house with a suitcase full of clothes, his birthday and Christmas presents and some GCSE revision books. See you in a few years, son, good luck with the exams!

You know he'll be at your parents' for a few hours and we'll miss him, go and pick him up, then regret it instantly, right?

Jokes aside, I'm just trying to enjoy this forced period at home. We're in unprecedented times. I just want everyone to be safe and happy while we're all going through it and hopefully it'll all be over soon. It makes you realize how many things you take for granted. I honestly think I'll burst into tears of joy the next time I go to a service station for a piss.

Wow. Not hugging your loved ones or visiting our favourite restaurant? You're excited to use service station lavatories again.

I'm fully used to being at home now, though. I'm in home mode. The itch to go out to work has gone. We've been writing the book and doing the podcast, so the creative outlet has been fulfilled. I'm a full-time Lego builder and cyclist now (bike guy!). I don't want to get too sentimental, but I'm actually dreading how much I'm going to miss being at home when I finally go away again. It's going to probably be worse than when Robin was first born, and definitely worse than when me and Rosie first got together and I worked away . . . But however bad it gets when I finally go back to work, I would a hundred per cent prefer it to lockdown . . .

Things You'll Miss . . .

Apologies if that title has made this chapter sound a bit doom and gloom and like some sort of pregnancy self-help book, because it's not, it's really not.

Thank God for that.

It's more of a guide to what you'll miss rather than how to prepare yourself. Although I suppose I could quickly go over a few things here . . .

First of all, children are genuinely wonderful. They have this magical ability to make you forget your problems and they possess the incredible skill of bringing a grin to your face no matter how sad you feel. I'm talking more about your own children here – other people's children are usually very annoying. Like you love them and you enjoy their company, but truth be told they're not officially yours and you can see straight through their bullshit. Luckily they're not your responsibility, you have enough of that as it is.

Yeah, other people's kids can fuck off.

There really is no other feeling like having a baby. The love you feel for them is incredible. Little do you know when this baby arrives that your world will never, LITERALLY never be the same again.

Here's a question we received from a naive couple about to have a baby. I say naive not in a condescending way, rather in an understanding way, as if you're a parent then you've been there. We're all guilty of being slightly naive before our baby comes along.

Hi Rosie and Chris,

My wife is pregnant with our first baby which is due in May.

I was wondering what things do you miss/are you unable to do any more after becoming parents that you didn't realize you would? So things that aren't immediately obvious, e.g. sleep.

I would love some advance warning. Thanks. Much appreciated,

Rhys

OK, so I could just jump straight in at the deep end here and reply EVERYTHING! But I feel that would be a tad cruel. So instead Chris and I have devised a little bullet-point list with some definite things you will have to wave goodbye to. Strap in, Rhys.

Dear reader, before you read this please remember that babies are fantastic, lush and lovely. I personally wouldn't give mine up

*for the world, but they're hard flipping work and your life will never be the same again . . . ***

I'd like to add I wouldn't give our son up either but would also still like to invite cash offers.

- **Sleep** is absolutely top of the shop. Not just the amount of sleep, but also the ability to sleep when you want – being able to stay up and watch telly as late as you would like is also out of the window. If you still want to carry out your daily duties as a functioning human being then no more late nights, I'm afraid . . . more about this later!
- **Being able to eat a full meal without having to give any of it away.** Our little boy could have exactly the same meal as me on his plate yet he will still try to steal most of mine. I once did this back to him and he had a monumental breakdown. We now share everything (begrudgingly) as it's just too emotionally draining.

I can't remember the last time I got to finish a bag of crisps. And pizza. He eats his then starts on mine! I'm going to have to resort to eating exclusively vindaloos when he's about, but I know he'd develop a taste for it . . . then his farts would be unbearable.

- **Eating a treat in front of your child** or drinking a cup of juice in front of them – forget about it. They will want it, they will steal it. If they can see it, it's no longer yours. Forever! I eat most of my biscuits inside the kitchen cupboard. It's nowhere near as enjoyable as it used to be, but needs must.

I have been known to eat a Creme Egg in the toilet and once ate a Victoria sponge in the shower. The shower wasn't on, I just stood in the cubicle and closed the door, fully clothed, and ate the slice of cake with my hands. Like a winner.

- **Pissing/shitting alone.** I've tried numerous diversion tactics over the years but to no avail. It would appear that as soon as your arse hits the seat it is in their minds the perfect moment to tell you something. It's always pointless information and it usually ends up with me having to do something, thus cutting my precious toilet alone time short.

Yep, he came and showed me some Lego he'd built while I was sitting on the toilet just yesterday!

- **Bathing alone.** Same as above but they usually hop in, with ALL their toys.

And inevitably you'll miss bathing in water that doesn't have toddler piss in it. Sometimes, Robin and I will be in the bath together and you can tell when he's having a sneaky wee in it. He'll stop talking and kind of look off into the distance for a second. And I'll say, 'Are you having a wee?' He used to deny it, then he started denying it and then laughing, then he started admitting it and laughing, THEN he started shouting 'I'm having a wee' while doing it. It continued escalating until it got to the stage where he would actually choose not to have a wee in the toilet before his bath so he could wee in the bath with me in it. It's now reached an unprecedented level where he literally stands up in the bath we're sharing and pisses back into the water right in front of me. Absolutely feral.

- *Basically doing anything alone ever again.*

You have to literally steal yourself away like a spy if you want to watch a video on your phone that has swearing in it. Sometimes, if Robin and Rosie are doing something that takes just the two of them, videoing each other dancing or painting or something that basically doesn't need me, I will just go and sit in another room in silence for a bit. Just for a bit of quiet time. Sometimes I don't even take my phone. I'm considering inventing 'jobs' that need to be done in the loft and just going and sitting up there on the dusty floor for a bit of space.

- **Swearing or talking about anything adult-themed in your own home.** Gone are the days of airing your feelings! You have to learn to speak in code. Don't slag off your parents in front of your children either as they'll most likely tell them, and that just opens up a whole can of worms that you don't need.

To be fair, the amount of things we have to spell out in conversation now has really improved my overall literacy. You want to quickly know how to spell a swear word? I'm your man! It's actually helped with this book, to be honest. The most frustrating thing is when you're spelling something out or talking in code and your partner doesn't understand what you're getting at ... OR even worse, and this is the most common one, you start using code and your partner just talks normally and fucks the whole thing up! This usually happens when she's on her phone and only half listening:

Me – 'Rosie, when he goes to bed shall we O-R-D-E-R a C-U-R-R-Y?'

Rosie – 'YES! I'd love a curry!'

Me – 'Shit, man! Rosie!?'

Robin – 'CURRY! I want some popadums!! ... Shit, man!'

- *Having a tidy/clean house.*

Well, I can't comment on this because I gave that up when I married Rosie.

- *Watching what you want on the TV.* I've became obsessed with interior decorating and cookery shows as they're the only thing I can watch during the day without any swears!

Again, gave this up when I married Rosie.

- *Listening to music you want to listen to.*

Again . . . starting to see a pattern here, Rosie! I've lost track of how many times I will be out in the car listening to MY Spotify account and the music will quickly change to the *PJ Masks* Theme, CBeebies or Bette Midler because you and Robin are using the smart speaker at home, which is linked to, and I will say this again, MY SPOTIFY ACCOUNT. I almost crash the car attempting to change it back a thousand times then get an angry phone call telling me to listen to the radio.

- *'Popping' ANYWHERE.* Being unable to go any-where quickly without a screaming match becomes the new norm. Bribery will become your new best friend. You'll come out of all this like some sort of politician, striking up deals on a daily basis. Unfortunately, in our house this has recently backfired a little, as the other day Robin was actually bribing *me*, and I fell for it hook, line and sinker. I told him it was time to brush his teeth and he said, 'If you let me watch one more *Mr Men* I will be a good boy while you brush my teeth.' Little shit is catching on, dammit!

Basically have to factor some 'hostage negotiation time' into every trip. And on the subject of bribing, Rosie seems to have a 'do as I say, not as I do' policy. She can literally offer Robin chocolate, toys and a controlling stake in a Fortune 500 company to get in the car but if I dare to give him a single piece of Lego to stop him kicking off I'm 'spoiling him'.

- *A clean car.*

Again . . . gave this up a while ago. The sheer amount of shit that Rosie deposited in the door compartment of my old car was staggering. Murray Mint wrappers (some with half-sucked mints in them), chewed-up straws, apple cores, crisp packets, crisp packets with apple cores in, bottles, car park tickets, car park tickets with chewing gum in them. You name it, it was there. I genuinely went to pick my new car up from the dealership and the salesman said these words, 'Only problem is, it doesn't have compartments in the doors' – I nearly kissed him. And her face when she got in and realized it didn't have door compartments . . . it was like telling someone their hotel room didn't have a toilet. She never drives my car now, claiming that it's because she's worried she'll damage it, but I know it's really because there's nowhere for her to deposit her waste as she drives along sucking sweet after sweet like an old nana at the bingo.

Hahaha! Wrong. I just hate your car. And mine is absolutely nowhere near as bad as you're describing it here like.

- **_Your body._** This is more so for the ladies. Say hello to your new little shelf! Obviously, it goes without saying the human body is wonderful and I'm so grateful and amazed at the fact that my own body was able to grow and birth my beautiful baby boy, but for God's sake, could you not have allowed me to keep any parts of my pre-baby body? I think the only thing that didn't change was my nose! Don't even get me started on bloody bladder weakness, what a lovely little surprise that was.

Can't really comment on this apart from to say it's not a great idea, while your wife or partner is pregnant or still carrying baby weight, to loudly and proudly exclaim, 'I've lost half a stone even though I'm eating loads of takeaways!' It tends to cause a bit of friction.

- **Relaxing.** It's hard to switch off when you have kids.

You're now constantly 'on call' even when you're asleep, even when you're at work . . . probably even when you're dead. And the moment they disappear into another room and start 'playing quietly' is the moment you have to be most alert . . . because the little shits are up to something. They've found something or gained access to something that they shouldn't have. You now have two choices:

a) Enjoy the peace and silence for as long as it lasts and clean up the possible disaster area at a later point, or

b) Stand up now, go through and stop the disaster in its tracks, but knowing full well that you have also stopped any peace and quiet you were about to enjoy in its tracks. Choose wisely.

- **Clean windows.** Once your little one is walking by themselves you'll never look out of a window in your house without a manky, smarmy, *Titanic* sex scene-esque handmark on it.

Well, I'm never going to be able to look at those marks the same way again. Thanks for that!

- ***Having a sit-down three-course meal.*** Eating slowly and enjoying yourself in a restaurant are both a thing of the past, even when you are without your child, as you'll inevitably have to get back home for the babysitter or you'll get too excited like we do and have too much to drink before your meal and get tired and want an early night with a lie-in the next day.

You are now a 'dine and dash' family. Onlookers might be forgiven for thinking you're running away without paying the bill because you are in and out of there at such a speed. And you now have to profusely apologize to the waiters for the absolute STATE of the floor under your table and your kid's chair . . . or, do what we do and tidy it up yourself like you work there.

- ***Being able to glance at your phone without it being taken off you.*** Robin loves playing on my phone. Although you can get round this by never putting games on your phone, but then I end up having to quickly download them as we enter a restaurant just so we can eat in peace.

I deliberately have no games on my phone at all. I've told him, 'Games don't work on Daddy's phone.' He actually thinks my phone is worse than Rosie's even though it's the same model and you can still get YouTube Kids on it . . . sucker!

- ***Not feeling constantly guilty.*** I feel guilt every day. In fact, I can quite confidently say there's not a day gone by since our little boy's birth that I've not experienced some sort of guilt. I remember it started the day we brought him home from the hospital when I asked Chris: 'Do you think he's happy? Do you think he likes the house?' As if I asked that! He's the luckiest kid in the world! He's already better off than I ever was being born into his own room. Must be nice.

You feel like you need some time away from the kid, you feel guilty. You have the time away, you miss them, you feel guilty. You're with them and not playing with them enough, you feel guilty. You let them watch TV, you feel guilty. The list goes on and on and on . . .

- **Sticking to plans.** It's just so difficult getting out the house! You don't have the energy. Never before has lying on the sofa at the end of the day been so bloody inviting. You'll find that you're rarely on time for anything once you have a child. I always used to pride myself on being quite a punctual person until I had Robin; now I'm either extremely late or extremely early and there's no in-between. I tried not to be late so I started to get ready ridiculously early and make sure I'd leave the house at least an hour early, and I'd arrive places too soon, which is never a good idea because kids don't like to be in the same place for longer than an hour, so you've already shot yourself in the foot. It's a logistical nightmare. Constantly!

To be fair, I've always loved cancelling plans. If I can get out of a night out and stay in, I'm buzzing. I can safely say that in my life I have cancelled more nights out than I have actually gone on.

- *A leisurely stroll around the supermarket.*

Those days are gone. If they aren't crying, they're asking for everything in sight. We usually open stuff and let Robin eat it on the way round then scan the empty packets at the end like the shameful nearly thieves we are. You can't go wrong with a fresh white baguette and a punnet of grapes #DineandDash AKA supermarket lunch.

- *Hangover/sick days on the settee.* This right here is something I never fully took into consideration before having a child. I actually feel this may need its own little sub-chapter in the book. What do you reckon, Chris?

Ah yeah, definitely.

Stop Banging, I'm Hanging

Aaaah . . . all those wonderful sick days I took for granted before I had a child. How I miss them.

Those hours upon hours of lying on the sofa, watching daytime TV without a care in the world, surrounded only by my own misery and the occasional phone call from a friend retelling funny tales from the evening before or a work colleague calling to check up on me while I'm laid up in bed poorly, letting me know if the boss believed I was poorly or not and relaying any juicy gossip.

Longingly waiting for your mam to come home from work and bring you cans of Lilt and crisp sandwiches to make you feel better. They always did, didn't they?

I was once off school for a week and my mam went to the video shop and got me all of the *Star Wars* videos . . . Best. Week. Ever.

My mam was a nurse for almost fifteen years so she was hard to fool. When she actually believed that I or my siblings were poorly we couldn't quite credit our luck. Even to this day, if my mam suggests I go to see the doctor I do a little happy dance inside. 'She BELIEVES ME! She actually believes me! I AM poorly! I knew it!!' I've been known to cry in these moments, a mixture of really feeling unwell and the sheer exhaustion and self-belief in my fever all rolled into one.

Remember how smug you were when the doctor TOLD your mam to keep you off school. What a feeling!

Those carefree ill years were short-lived, and to be totally honest, I don't think I appreciated them enough at the time.

I remember what it was like in the days of long, long ago when you would feel a cold coming on: a little sneeze perhaps, or a slight headache, and you'd think, 'Oh, I'd best keep an eye on that. Maybe I'll plan a sick day off work? It'll only last a couple of days. I'm young, healthy and full of natural young energy and shit, I'll be right as rain in a few days of R and R!' What a smug little twat I was.

Say this cold struck on a Monday morning. I would call in sick to work or college, have a couple of days in the house and I'd be fighting fit come the weekend for my mate's birthday night out. Totally cured!

That's because you didn't get EMA (Education Maintenance Allowance), Rosie! You could afford to phone in sick to college. If I had a day off it cost me £10 a week! And my end-of-term £180 bonus. I'd drag myself to college in any state to keep that bad boy. I made more from college than I did from my fucking job at All:Sports.

You've always been a jammy little bastard, Ramsey. I never got EMA as my parents earned just over the threshold, yet I was still made to pay board! Totally swizzled I was.

Nowadays you need to add in a couple of kids, a full-time job, parental GUILT (I mentioned this before), a full-on adult life to run, a demanding husband, and that said little cold will be following you around for weeks.

Demanding?!

You can say goodbye to your mate's birthday night out now – you'll never be well enough for a drink on Friday. No chance! You'll be snotting all over the place and you'll more than likely get so run-down by it that you'll catch an eye infection to add insult to injury. Nobody wants to see a gooey, manky eye on their birthday. Oh dear God, no. You know that in order to recover you need to stay at home. It isn't worth having a drink either – you'll not even be able to taste it and that's just a waste of a bottle.

I'd suggest an early bath, but if your house is anything like mine, some little fucker will hear you running it and jump in before you get the chance to kindly and lovingly tell them to please piss off. (Actually, what is it with children refusing a bath when you want them to have one but they're all stripped off and diving in the second you start to run one for yourself?? Arseholes.)

I'd suggest having an early night, but those sacred three hours of time to yourself in an evening when you have been a little person's slave all day are just too precious to give up. If I'm lucky I can get three hours between Robin going to bed and my usual bedtime and I make the most of that time. I leave the dishes, I don't put toys away. I sit on my knackered arse and watch TV for three hours straight. I need it, please don't take it away from me by suggesting I go to bed early.

Yep. I get shouted at if I merely suggest going to bed before 10 p.m. and in the morning the house looks like students have taken up residence in a branch of Smyths Toys.

So, no doubt you'll numb yourself up on a dangerous concoction of Lemsip, ibuprofen and Berocca. You'll force yourself to stay awake watching shite TV all because you want to be by yourself and awake enough to enjoy it. Then you can look forward to being unnaturally woken up at daft o'clock in the morning by the little twat who gave you the said illness in the first place.

Cheers, son.

While we're on the subject.

Remember waking up naturally?

Like, without a screaming banshee child demanding to go downstairs and eat you out of house and home. How can anyone be that hungry at that time in the morning when they've literally just this second opened their eyes? What even are you? Robin literally opens his eyes and that's it. There's no relaxing in bed, taking his time to get up, reading a book . . . No, no, no. He is up, he is up and he is raring to go! I honestly reckon our Robin could run a half-marathon thirty seconds after he's opened his eyes. The kid's a lunatic.

Yep. Now, life is going to bed and thinking, 'Wonder what time I'll be woken up tomorrow morning. Hope it's after 6 a.m. at least . . . and hope there isn't TOO much shouting!'

In the days before the walking talking alarm clock that is our son, I'd wake up from a deep, uninterrupted, peaceful sleep as the sunlight hit the window, that gorgeous glow streaming into the bedroom. Can you remember? You'd have time to gather your thoughts and possibly doze for a few more minutes. You would plan your outfit, perhaps, or think of contacting a friend to see if they were free to meet for lunch.

Your partner is lying beside you, you turn to look at them, you stare at them like a person who has lost their mind. You are so in love with this person that you think your heart might explode out of your chest. You move closer towards them, breathe them in. That gorgeous morning smell of the person you love. Chris used to smell like toast. Honestly! His neck smelt like toast and it was LUSH! I haven't smelt him in the morning for a while now, so I have no idea if he still does or not. Might have a little sniff tomorrow morning, if I can be arsed? I'll see.

For the record, I'm perfectly fine with no longer being sniffed first thing on a morning.

You would think about possibly initiating sex. You're at that stage of the relationship when sex is never off the table, the more the better.

Morning sex. Wowee. Let's all take a second to remember the wonderment of morning sex. Hot diggedy dog! I frigging used to LOVE morning sex. No end-of-day bloat, still half-asleep so there doesn't need to be a huge amount of effort involved, shower once you're done. Amazing. Now, I honestly can't remember the last time I partook in morning sex. Probably about five years ago when we conceived our little boy. God, that's grim.

The married couples with young kids that you see in films still have morning sex. Who even are these people? It's just not feasible. Fuck you all.

Reasons why I no longer have morning sex (these are my personal views but I'm pretty sure Chris would also agree . . .):

1. I cannot be arsed. Purely and simply do not have the energy.
2. Don't touch me – you smell like you are an actual dead person.

I'm a big fan of a pre-morning-sex teeth-brush . . . or at least a quick mouthwash.

3. I'm pretty sure we had an argument last night before bed about something. I can't remember what it was about exactly, but I remember that I was fucking livid and I'm definitely in the right, so don't you dare try to touch me without apologizing first. Oh, and a cup of coffee in bed, please. Thank you.
4. I'm not pissed. Sex is better these days when we're drunk.
5. We are never up before our son.
6. He is literally lying in between us. I ain't no biology teacher, but I'm pretty sure you need to be able to touch each other to enjoy the art of sex. Also,

I think trying anything with him in the bed with us would be against the law and extremely damaging to him.

7. I cannot be fucking arsed.

It's not only morning sex and waking up naturally that has gone out of the window, but hitting snooze on the alarm clock has too. Have you tried snoozing a kid? Not an option, babes. They don't take it well, trust me. Kids are dangerous first thing in the morning. They're energetic, spontaneous, rude and have no care for you or your unwillingness to get out of bed. Resistance is futile and will usually result in a kick to the stomach or a fart in the face – or is it just mine that does this? Great.

Can I just take this opportunity to say that people who snooze their alarms should be thrown into the sea? Absolute torture to be lying next to. It should be illegal.

I also didn't think I'd ever see the day that I would stop drinking at 11 p.m. on a weekend, the sole reason being that children don't know what a weekend is. They know they are off school, but they have no idea that it is also supposed to be a day off for their parents. But days off don't exist any more – you just don't get to escape the house and go to work.

'I have to get up with the bairn tomorrow' becomes your new turn of phrase while out with your childless friends. Luckily the ones with children will fully understand and you'll all usually share a taxi together, miserable at the looming human alarm coming your way at 6 a.m. You have to get up and actually care for someone the next day and you are all aware that trying to do it with a foggy head is never a good idea. Doesn't mean you'll ever learn from your mistakes, mind, because guaranteed come next Saturday night you'll be doing the same all over again. I don't think you'd mind as much if kids were remotely grateful, but they're not. They have no idea of the world of pain that is caring for them with a hangover.

Kids know when you're hung-over, they can sense it. Even though they have no concept of what alcohol is, or what being drunk is, or how you feel the following morning . . . they fucking know. They sense a weakness in you, a lethargy, they can somehow tell that you're not operating at full capacity, so they dial their dickhead-o-meter up to full. They take an age to decide what to have for breakfast, they change their mind halfway through making it. Robin will decide HE wants to pour the milk into his porridge and it'll go everywhere. The minute you sit down he wants something else. He can tell I'm flagging and he wants to break me.

Sometimes I'll attempt to have a sneaky nap if me and him are sitting on the sofa watching a movie and the little shit will physically open my eyes with his fingers . . . like that scene in *A Clockwork Orange* where they are making him watch ultra-violent footage, only Robin's torture video of choice is *Toy Story*. Somehow, his enjoyment of the film is ruined if I'm not sitting there wide-eyed taking it all in too. It's just not worth it. If I know I'm looking after Robin on my own in the morning, I very rarely get pissed the night before. It's torture. Honestly, if the FBI happen to be reading this, if you want to interrogate a suspect, forget Guantanamo and all that, send them here after a heavy night and sit them on the sofa with Robin while he shouts along to *The Mr Men Show* . . . they'll crack in minutes.

This I why I am now a MASSIVE advocate for DAYTIME DRINKING. Daytime drinking is the best.

Get a beer in your hand by 2 p.m. and you'll be hammered by 5 p.m., eating a curry or a pizza by 7 p.m., asleep by 9 p.m., up at 6 a.m. fresh as a daisy (albeit stinking of curry or garlic)!

You have to really fuck up to be hung-over the next day after daytime drinking. As long as your last drink is before that pizza or curry, you're laughing, mate. Thank me later.

Chris calls it daytime drinking. I call it 'avoiding your family drinking'.

I have always had a massive phobia of phoning in sick. I always think no one believes me. Even to this day when I tell Rosie I'm not well I assume she thinks I'm full of shit.

'The boy who cried wolf' comes to mind here, Christopher . . .

I once phoned in to All:Sports after a MASSIVE night out at a place called Tall Trees near Middlesbrough. It was an all-you-can-drink nightclub and I drank so much knock-off WKD Blue my poo the next day was green! No lie. And I know you're thinking, 'Was it a little bit green, Chris?' No. It was FULLY GREEN. Like green playdough.

Hooooooowwwwwwoooooh!!! There's no way it was fluorescent green, Chris.

Anyway, I was HANGING and I made the biggest mistake phoning in sick . . . I was honest! I spoke to my manager (who was a bell-end) and said to him, 'I'm feeling really hung-over, any chance you don't need me today so I can stay off?' – what an idiot. He obviously said absolutely not and made my entire day a living nightmare. He made me organize the stockroom . . . I almost vomited into a pair of Nike Air Max. All for £2.75 an hour. Idiot.

NEVER tell your boss you're hung-over!! Lost a leg, dislocated a shoulder! Anything other than hung-over. Rookie mistake there, babe.

All of this said . . . Huge congratulations on your upcoming little bundle of joy! It's honestly the best thing you'll ever do.

I know we haven't really sold it like that, but Robin is genuinely the best thing that's ever happened to us. We love that little boy more than any other human being on this planet, we wouldn't change our little turd burglar for anything.

Annoyingly and inexplicably, he is. Congrats!

Living with a Comedian . . .

First and foremost I thought marrying a comedian would be a right laugh – a laugh a minute, you could say. Turns out I was completely wrong.

Comedians aren't always funny. I know, I couldn't believe it either. Imagine my horror once I finally found this out? 'Hang on a minute? You're not always telling jokes and making people laugh? No way, I didn't sign up for this!'

Don't get me wrong, there is a lot of laughter in our marriage. It sounds weird, but most of our married life is Chris and I laughing at a funny situation or story, then for the next few weeks Chris retelling said story to all of our family and friends to see if it gets the same reaction. True story, he's been doing this since I first met him. He will write whatever was funny down in the notes section of his phone, then if it's remotely funny he will retell it. If it gets the same reaction as it did with him and me then the story will go into Chris's next stand-up show. If it doesn't he'll either stick with it until it does or it'll get scrapped and never spoken of again.

STOP LETTING PEOPLE BEHIND THE CURTAIN, ROSIE!

'Wow! That's a really cool process! How marvellous! I never knew that's what they did!'

Yes, it is, isn't it? It's very interesting! I never knew it was the way comedians work either, well, this comedian anyway. Ooh, how fascinating, I thought the first few times I noticed him doing it. He's so talented! Gosh, I'm so attracted to him, this talented, funny human that I've bagged for myself! That feeling didn't last very long. Unfortunately it's not so interesting and fascinating when you happen to spend most of your time with the person who is constantly conducting the human laughter experiment, and you're having to hear said funny story being repeated dozens and dozens of times, over and over again exactly the same way.

It's called 'getting your money's worth', and you are one lucky little ducky!

I often wonder if our friends think I'm an absolute cold-hearted bitch because unfortunately by the time the story gets to them I don't actually have any laughter left in me. I just can't bring it to the surface, no matter how hard I try. It's just gone.

See, used up all your laughter! How many other wives can say that? I'm the gift that keeps on giving.

Chris is very funny, it's true, and he's extremely talented, but often it's like watching *Friends* on Comedy Central. I love it, but I've just had enough, you know?

Errm, one of the most successful sitcoms in history, so, I'll have that compliment, THANK YOU.

I'm not sure if this is how other comedians work as Chris is the only one I've ever been married to (thank God). But I'd actually be interested to know. I'm not sure if any comedians will read this (I highly doubt it), but if you are, could you please let me know? Or maybe your partners could drop me a little DM just to let me know that I'm not alone in this really strange world. Oooh, I could start like a comedy WAG group! We could go to gigs together and heckle our partners from the back of the theatre. Ah, that would be funny, I'd really enjoy that. *It's not as funny when you've heard it NINETY-FOUR times, mate!!' 'That never happened!! Don't believe him!' 'BULLSHIIIIITTT!'* Actually, that's one thing I'll give Chris – he's never lied about any of his stand-up. He's often embellished a little for comedic effect, but they are very much things and situations that have happened in his life.

I invite you and whoever you can wrangle together to come and try this . . . I will crucify you all. (No podcast fans allowed as they will side with you, actually.)

For clarity, just in case you happen to have seen Chris live, yes, I did shit myself in Nando's when I was five months pregnant. I was extremely constipated and it was a horrific accident which I'm still absolutely mortified about, and yes, I did get a little bit of my own poo on my sandal and have to leave it at the side of the road at the back of the restaurant car park.

All Growed Up LIVE DVD still available.

Such an awful day that was, which would probably never have been spoken about again if I'd been sensible in my life partner choice. Bet you wouldn't have heard a teacher going into work and telling his colleagues about his poor pregnant, constipated wife having an accident in their local Nando's. No, he wouldn't have wanted to embarrass me like that – he'd have had some respect for me. Showed me a little kindness, spared me my blushes. Nope. Not a comedian husband. These little vultures see everything as an opportunity for a good old tale to make all the simple folk laugh. Unfortunately, in their eyes you are no longer a wife – you're a character in their messed-up comedy where the world is a stage and the fact that you managed to shit yourself while out for chicken – well, you were just playing to his tune there, my love. Like putty in his filthy jester hands.

Got to pay for all those sofas somehow!

I can only blame myself for telling him in the first place, to be honest. Should have kept that shit to myself, literally.

That story nearly broke me, not going to lie, especially when I heard it live on stage for the first time. 'Bloody hell, he's really doing it . . . He's actually telling them about when I shat myself. Oh God, they know it's me, they know I'm his wife. There's a frigging camera in my face.' Oh yes, it was also recorded for the DVD. Forgot to mention that little nugget, didn't I? My darling husband, love of my life Christopher Ramsey, thought it would be a great idea to not only

tell the thousands of people who had already come to see
him live, but he also decided that the world needed to
know of my incontinence too. Great! Cheers, babe! Love
you too.

More people have already pre-ordered this book than bought
the DVD . . . so you have just told even more people who might
not have known about it . . . just saying.

That was the point I realized that I was in really deep and
nothing in our marriage was sacred any more. After that live
show he knew he was on to a winner with me, reason being
that luckily for him I'm actually quite good at being able to
laugh at myself. It really does take an awful lot for me to get
embarrassed. Hence how I'm able to write in a published book
about shitting myself when I was completely sober, during the
day, in my twenties.

Late twenties.

We started our podcast not long after Chris had regaled thousands of people with this jolly tale on his UK tour. It helped,
to be honest, because I have tons of embarrassing stories just
like that, so I thought, 'Sod it! Might as well open this little
treasure chest a bit more, eh?' Plus it was finally an opportunity for me to be able to answer him back and embarrass him as
much as he has embarrassed me and our close circle over the
years. Only problem is it's all gone a little better than we first

anticipated and now we've ended up with literally no secrets between us, which is refreshing in a way, but it's also a lot like washing your dirty knickers and kegs in public. I think we may need to rethink this plan? Either that or start using code names . . .

I think we are well past that . . . plus you just told everyone that genius plan.

I have to say that if Rosie wasn't able to laugh at herself, you would not be reading this book now. It would never have worked, as you might have already guessed. And to be fair, she can give as good as she gets, which is why the podcast is so fun for me. Even if no one was listening it's just so much fun to sit and slag each other off and have a laugh with it, in a way that you couldn't really do in day-to-day life without being drunk or making all of your mates you're on the night out with feel uncomfortable.

Rosie has told me multiple times that living with a comedian isn't all it's cracked up to be, but do you know what, I reckon it's a lot easier than . . .

Living with an Influencer

Hey, do you like taking photos of your partner? YOU DO!? Well, you're in luck! She's got loads of followers on Instagram now, so you're going to have to take 300 at a time whenever she's trying on a new dress, leaving for a night out or just popping to the shops!

Do you like filming things? Not too keen on that? Well, hard lines, mate! She'll randomly come into the office while you're working wearing an Elsa from *Frozen* dress and a blonde wig and demand you stand and film her as she improvises a song about getting a fucking blue tick on Instagram.

I did it in one shot and it got over a quarter of a million views. F you. Oh, and I look banging as Elsa.

And once that is over, you can enjoy sitting in the same room as she edits that video! You can listen to the entire audio in small segments on repeat for about an hour until it's done. THEN she'll put it online and watch it again about fifty times for no reason at all. ENJOY!

She may be an annoying influencer, but she is a brilliant wife and mother and she's also a fantastic cook, and you'll regret all of the above grievances and feel like a bastard when she cooks you a beautiful nutritious meal . . . THAT IS UNTIL you are made to stand looking at your meal as it goes cold because she's having a fucking photoshoot with it!

'Move that rubbish in the background, put that wine bottle over there, get a nicer glass out!' THE FUN NEVER ENDS!

Make your own bloody meals then, you ungrateful chump! I bet Delia Smith's husband doesn't go on like this.

Enjoy being safe in your own home? Lounging in comfort away from public eyes? THINK AGAIN! Be ready to be in the background of videos in your pyjamas, unwashed, unshaven, hair messy and sometimes with that little piss droplet you get on grey sweatpants. YOU WILL NEVER BE SAFE AGAIN!

I'll be sure to keep my ad revenue well away from your bank account from now on then, babes. #ad #Mine;-D

Micro-Mamar-Managing

I thought we would take this opportunity to make you all, dear readers, aware of a terrible illness that can befall your parents when you yourself have children. Let this serve as a warning, if you will, for later on in your parental life. A warning for parents/in-laws/grandparents/aunts/uncles who may or may not fall victim to the incurable (many have tried to cure it) illness of the wearing of . . . ***Rose-Tinted Glasses***.

Unfortunately for us, my mother (Sandra, known as 'Mamar' to all her grandchildren) has suffered terribly with rose-tinted glasses syndrome for over ten years now. It started when my older sister had her first son and it's gradually got worse with each grandchild.

Now I must add here that I love my mother to death – she is an INCREDIBLE Mamar to her four grandsons – but unfortunately for us, her long-suffering children, these glasses mean business and her viewing of the past through them is constant and relentless.

The main symptom of rose-tinted glasses is misremembering vital details of your children's childhood and looking back on the time very differently from all your children who were also there and can attest too. Your mother will have you believing that you and your siblings were angels sent from heaven, who never misbehaved and slept like 20-year-old Labradors.

If you're unlucky like me it can start to rear its ugly head during your actual pregnancy, but usually and in milder cases it doesn't properly develop until the four- to five-day-old mark. That's when it really kicks in. It starts as standard bits of passive-aggressive advice then moves on to backing up these bits of advice with flat-out LIES from the past . . .

'Should he be wearing that many layers, Rosie? It's boiling out today!'

'He looks freezing, Rosie. Look at his lips, look! Look! They're blue! Here, put this blanket round him.'

'You should have extra blankets, you know? At all times, I never left the house without an extra blanket for you three.'

'Ah, Rosie, it's boiling! Take his hat off him, let his skin get some vitamin D! Poor bairn's going to have a deficiency! I ALWAYS made sure you lot got fifteen minutes of sun every day.'
(Sandra Winter's Greatest Hits circa 2014)

Fifteen minutes of sun EVERY DAY?!? In the north of England? HOW? Did we have a sunbed I wasn't aware of, Mother?

This was all in one day, might I add. Exhausting. You can't win. You literally cannot win. You are brand new to this parenting malarkey and she's done it three times already, and you were one of them! You're OK? You turned out all right? Right? Everything she's saying must be true. Why would she suggest it otherwise?

Nobody else is offering advice, so I'd better do everything she says. I just wish she didn't say so flipping much . . .

Here are some other examples of how the rose-tinted glasses syndrome might present itself from your own mother.

'Snacks weren't a thing when you's were little. You got three square meals a day and that was it. Cakes and sweets are for birthdays, Rosie! Not random Tuesday afternoons! Tut!' (Sandra Winter 2015)

It's funny, that, Mam, because I can guarantee you that I could go into the loft now and get out the big box of old photos and find about twenty of them in which one of us is eating a bag of crisps or a biscuit – not at a mealtime, might I add, but as a SNACK!

'Ah, have you got the telly on for him again, have you?'

Wow. Really, Sandra? This is the one that always floors me the most because I have it on good authority (from my dad) that I used to sit in front of the telly with a bowl of chips. (Made in the deep-fat frier. How unhealthy, Sandra!) No wonder we didn't eat any snacks! You were too busy clogging up our innocent little arteries with delicious lardy goodness!

I did bloody love those chips, I have to say.

Dad told me that I'd eat my chips while watching the Care Bears ON LOOP. Just episode after episode, rotting my little brain.

'Rosie, there's loads of stuff you don't need on these window-sills. Why don't you put it all away? The bairn's trying to climb up and get it, man!'

Time, Mam – not got much time at the minute, you know? You remember, right? When you had three kids running round and the house was upside down? It was. I remember. It never bothered us. In fact it was comforting not living in a pristine house, you did a great job! Stop lying to yourself that your house was always spotlessly clean!

'You three never threw tantrums like this when you were little.'

See again, Mam, funny you say that, because instantly I remember – and quite vividly, actually – the day my little brother Kevin split the back of my head open by whacking me full force with a metal door handle he found on the bathroom window-sill, in your bathroom. Hmmmm, so strange . . . Ah, if only you'd taken your own rose-tinted advice then and put stuff away in its rightful place. Might have saved yourself an afternoon in Shields A&E.

'You shouldn't give in to their demands so much! Let them cry it out!'

I once demanded that you let me empty out my wardrobe to put a table and chair in there so I could pretend I had my own office room. I remember you saying to Dad that you didn't care as long as I was out of your hair for a few hours.

Now, you need to realize I am saying this very much in jest. (Well, sort of. She'll be reading this so I best be careful! Love you, Mam! xxx) But I just felt that if you're reading this and you have a baby on the way, you can at least be prepared for it, as it will happen. Mothers can't help themselves.

The shocking thing is that I fully intend to do the same when my children are older. In fact I think it's a rite of passage we just have to endure.

The one thing you mustn't do is retaliate. Oooooh, they don't like that. No, they don't like that at all . . . I've tried and failed miserably, but annoyingly I know all this advice always comes from a place of love and care.

Most importantly, though, you must try your very best to

never ever piss off or fall out with your parents or in-laws. Not only is it an absolute ball-ache emotionally, but it will most definitely impact your **Childcare**.

That's right. Unless you are lucky enough to have a live-in nanny (THE DREAM!) or extremely lovely family/friends who will happily look after your children on the regs, you can't be jeopardizing that sort of help.

If you want to be drinking a Malbec with your best friends in your favourite pub, then I strongly suggest you just smile and nod.

Say it with me now . . . *smile AND nod.*

Can I just take this opportunity to say that I absolutely LOVE Sandra and I thank her daily for the help and support she gives us? She looks after Robin, she cleans our house and sometimes even does our washing! So, 'Smile and nod' is now what I will be saying to YOU, Rosie, every time you and your mam start having a massive row and she ends up leaving the house in a huff because – let's not lie here – you two love a row! The arguments never last too long and they are always best mates again after, but the problem is Rosie and Sandra are too alike. They are almost the same person so they sometimes rub each other up the wrong way.

I happen to be a massive fan of the rose-tinted glasses syndrome that Sandra suffers from as it has a by-product that she has called 'Side with Chris Over Rosie in Almost Every Argument-itis'. For years I have listened to people slag off their mothers-in-law – it's a well-trodden area in stand-up comedy. I couldn't believe my luck when I got landed with Sandra. She will literally fight my corner against Rosie like I'm her own son. It's amazing. It annoys Rosie and I win the argument. Jackpot! If I was a rapper Sandra would be that other rapper on stage with me who just shouts 'YEAH!' after everything I say. She's my in-house hype man!

My mam and dad are, obviously, great too and I have to thank them for the support we get from them as grandparents . . . Not sure if they'll read this, though, so I could go full out and slag them off . . . but then again they get enough of that in my stand-up.

They don't really suffer from rose-tinted glasses in the same way that Rosie's mam does. They do have that weird thing of claiming that I didn't misbehave as much as I did or just flat out denying something that I tell them I remember so clearly. Maybe they just have shit memories? Who knows . . .

What both sets of parents – and most people of that generation that I know – DEFINITELY do is claim that they 'never watch TV during the day', yet whenever I go to either of their houses the TV is constantly on, playing old episodes of *Tipping Point* or *The Chase*. And when I walk in they always loudly state, 'I've just this second popped the TV on. I never have it on during the day!' – WELL, you just happen to have 'popped' it on every single time I come round during the day. I'm starting to think you POP it on when you wake up and then POP it off when you go to sleep.

Why are you lying about it? Who gives a shit if you watch TV during the day? They honestly react the way I used to when my parents would come into my room and catch me looking at photos of naked women on my first ever PC:

'I just opened it up, I didn't know what it was! My mate sent me it! Honest!'

You're retired, do whatever you want during the day. We have Netflix, Amazon Prime, YouTube, millions of channels – watch away! When I'm retired I shudder to imagine the amount of shit there will be to watch . . . I'll be surprised if I even see my grandkids.

But no, my mam and dad rarely bring out the rose-tinted glasses when it comes to my childhood. In fact, pop to their house for a cuppa and they will happily regale you with tale after tale of times I was almost accidentally killed or maimed by them as a child. They love it!

Here's the highlights:

• They regularly left the toddler gate at the TOP of the stairs open yet kept the BOTTOM one closed, even when I was upstairs. Meaning that on the one occasion that I ran across the landing and fell down the stairs my tumble was broken by a white metal mesh that I almost minced myself through.

• My mam once cut a cake with a massive knife that basically resembled a sword and left it RIGHT NEXT TO me in my highchair while she walked across the kitchen with the cake. She glanced back to see me holding the knife and attempting to lick the cake from it/give myself a forked tongue.

• I was once on my dad's shoulders walking along the promenade on holiday when he spotted a mate of his from work, in the same Spanish resort as us – imagine his excitement! My dad started shouting 'Barry! Barry! Barry!' at the top of his lungs and sprinting towards him, so giddy that he failed to notice the metal sign he was running directly under. The sign hit me full in the face and cleaned me off his shoulders like a WWE wrestler clothes-lining someone from the top rope. I fell through the air, about to impact on the pavement below, but my dad managed to make this WORSE by grabbing my ankle and pulling my leg up. What he in fact did was create a perfect whip crack between my head and the pavement. The noise of the crack followed by my hysterical screaming apparently reverberated around the entire beach and promenade for everyone to hear, including the man who looked a bit like, but actually wasn't, fucking Barry.

Thankfully we all laugh about these things now, because I turned out fine, and well, you have to really. Robin is currently spending his entire childhood with no front teeth and not a day goes by when I don't think about how the stories of that are going to haunt us all in later life . . . Christ, I hope he doesn't do a podcast . . . or a book.

Who Will Die First?

Dear Chris and Rosie,

I saw an article recently where an elderly couple took their own lives as one was terminally ill and they didn't want to live on without each other.

Me and my wife always discuss who would want to be the one to die first. Neither of us would want to die last and be left without the other one.

As such, I ask you who would you want to die first, and who would struggle the most being left behind?

Many thanks

Tim and Ali

What an utterly grim question, but luckily for you we enjoy utterly grim questions and topics. We've had a similar conversation ourselves recently, because let's face it, death is something that will inevitably come to us all.

Last year Chris and I made a will. I know what you're thinking . . . Why? You're both so young! Isn't that just what old people need to do? Well, I'll be totally honest with you here, I thought the same too. But I was randomly chatting to someone I know and the topic of wills came up. She told me that a friend of hers' husband had tragically died and all of their household money was in his name. His wife was unable to access any of their money. She couldn't use his cash card or pay any of their bills, and she ended up having to sell her car to pay for her shopping as it took so long to sort out with the bank.

Not going to lie to you, this put the fear of God into me, because up until this year I wasn't actually working and all our money was in Chris's name. (I say ours – it was really Chris's, but being married it's also mine.)

I'd just recently purchased a new car and I really liked it, and I didn't fancy having to sell it to pay for my online Tesco delivery should the inevitable happen. (Sorry, Chris.) So I thought it best that we go and get everything sorted, you know, just in case.

Hey, at least you're being honest.

We were shown to the 'will room' at the solicitors. I don't think it's actually called that, but it was proper depressing, so it'll always be etched in my memory as the will room. Picture the longest table imaginable in the smallest room, one window, and those horrible strip lights on the polystyrene-type tiles. The walls looked like they hadn't seen a paintbrush in over twenty years, but there were posh bottles of water and a plate of biscuits, so not all bad, I suppose.

It all starts off quite nice: 'This is a sensible decision. It'll give you great peace of mind for the future . . .' Then the mood very quickly changes once you get down to the actual nitty-gritty of it all.

I'm sure Chris will expand more on this as the whole thing really affected him a lot more than it did me (he doesn't like talking about serious life things, as you may have already guessed).

The element of the will that really caught me off guard was the 'What if' section – i.e., where does your money go in every possible scenario:

Chris dies – money goes to Rosie and Robin.

Rosie dies – nothing really changes as I don't cause much of a dent financially. They'll probably miss my home-made fish and chips, but that's about it. Oh, and all my potted plants would definitely take a hit water-wise.

They'd go straight in the skip, and the chippy round the corner is decent, to be fair.

Chris and Rosie die – this one really got me. I can't imagine Robin having to live without both of us. It really upset me, just having to think about it and putting plans in place in case it ever happened.

He would obviously get all our moneybags, but not till he turns 25. The option was either 18 or 25. Not being funny, but imagine inheriting all your parents' money when you're

18 years old! You'd go berserk! I mean, it doesn't even have to be a lot. Even if it was a couple of grand, I doubt you'd invest it wisely. I'd probably have done something daft like take my whole college class to Ibiza for the weekend.

A mate of mine got £10,000 on the day of his eighteenth birthday as compensation for knocking his teeth out at the age of seven in a playground. He went to the cash machine at midnight the day before his eighteenth birthday and printed a statement out with £10,000 on it as a keepsake . . . which he needed as proof it was ever there, because he spent it all in two months!

The next option was . . .

Chris, Rosie AND Robin die . . . Is it weird that my first thought about this horrific scenario is actually 'That's more like it! All of us together in one go! Nice and easy, and we'd cope better all together, I reckon'?

Bit annoyed that I agree with this . . .

Obviously with this option we had to leave our money somewhere. We were happy to leave it to our parents, but then the fact that they might not still be around by the time this happened meant it would then go to our siblings. Chris doesn't have any, whereas I have two. It's mostly his hard-earned cash, so he wanted to choose some of his mates and it all got a bit too complicated, so we decided to give it to our parents then once they die we'll change it! Phew! Got there in the end! Sorry to be so graphic (probably the wrong word?), but it all came flooding back to me there!

Definitely the wrong word ... as if you're writing a bloody book!

Moral of the story – wills are depressing A F. My advice would be to just write a little note of who you want to have your money and to look after your kids in your knicker drawer, and you're sorted, I reckon. They're really expensive too! And they make you feel unbelievably sad and after the meeting you get home and cuddle your children/car for hours.

OK, Rosie obviously didn't listen to the MASSIVE bit of the will meeting where they explained IN GREAT DETAIL that this kind of thing isn't legally binding and the government will end up getting all of your money, so please disregard what she just said.

Just do what my mam used to do. In her wisdom she would write a little will note out every time we went on holiday and leave it on the kitchen counter. It basically said that if anything happened to her she would want her parents to look after us. I'm not even sure my dad was before them, you know. I don't think he could be trusted with all three of us without my mam's supervision! He'll read this and call me and argue this very point, but I'm with Sandra on this one, he'd have been shite. We'd never have brushed our teeth and we'd have been lucky to see a bath once a month. Obviously, love you, Dad, but aye. You'd have been a shite single dad.

Again, notes aren't legally binding, don't do this . . . but I agree that Derek would have been shite. Sorry, Deggzy.

Also, what a depressing way to start a holiday?!

'You packed the travel plugs, Sandra?'

'Yeah!'

'Got the traveller's cheques?'

'Yes, Derek, you saw me pack those!'

'OK . . . left your morbid death note on the kitchen counter?'

'Shite, I'll do that now!'

Obviously, money and wills aside, neither Chris nor I would want to be left without the other because, you know, we love each other and that, but we did come to the conclusion that I (Rosie) would most likely, definitely, absolutely cope better in this situation.

I feel I was forced to this conclusion, but whatevs . . .

Now, this may have been a different answer before we had a child because we both lived very independently alone before marriage and our little boy. However, since the birth of our now 4-year-old son and having witnessed Chris getting Robin ready for school in the morning (not a pretty sight), I would constantly worry about his wellbeing from my grave. Rolling back and forth all day and night, I would be. I'd make sure that my mam/mother-in-law/sister/nana/auntie/cousins and friends were all given individual letters explaining that Robin may not survive in the sole care of Chris. He would be loved beyond measure and showered with endless amounts of Lego, but he'd be dressed in clothes three times too small and his toenails would be able to open the front door from the back sitting room. Me poor bairn!!

We would have LOADS of Lego, to be fair.

It's true – after four long years of co-parenting, Chris still can't seem to manage to leave the house without having to fucking ask me where something is.

He seems to have no clue as to where our child's clothes live or which bottle Robin likes to drink from, and don't even get me started on coats and shoes. Fuck me, it's like he's a stranger from an au pair agency who's come to help out for the day and take Robin to school. Utterly useless. Mind you, an au pair would do a better job.

You couldn't afford my au pair day rate!

I blame myself, to be honest.

I've always just 'done it'. I've found it a lot easier to get up earlier and pack Robin's bag myself. I leave his clothes out in little piles so Chris can just pick them up and put them on him. If I'm out I leave little notes with instructions on (as per Chris's request – useless bugger). It's absolutely my fault that Chris is so incapable of being a responsible adult and sorting out a young human for a simple day at the park.

He needs far too much stuff! We're going to the local park, not trekking in the fucking Andes!

I questioned his inability once. Here's how the exchange went . . .

'What I don't understand, Chris, is how you have no idea where anything is kept or what he might need for the day! Do you not have eyes? You watch me do this almost every single day. How have you not picked up any of this information?'

'I just assumed you liked doing it, so I've never bothered learning, to be honest, babe.'

LIKED doing it?? LIKED?! What?? There's zero liking involved, mate! If I didn't do it Robin would be walking around with his trousers barely covering his ankles and drinking out of your hands from the local toilet taps!!! (This is an exaggeration. I'm sure you'd have bought him a drink from a shop. At least I hope so. Chris? Please tell me you haven't ever let him drink out of your hands at a toilet tap?)

I'd washed them!

Chris will of course deny all of this. Just like my own dad, he likes to live in this imaginary world where he's a really capable dad (again, sorry Dad if you're reading this, but you all love to do this when in fact you're all pretty inept).

What he'll do is bring up that one time that he left me in bed and took Robin out for the day with his friend Carl and didn't need any help from me.

That's happened twice!

Just to clarify, reader, this was approximately three months ago. Robin was fully toilet trained, holding a proper conversation and dressing himself (sort of). Well done, babe, pat on the back.

Well, firstly, thank you for that well-deserved pat on the back, I shall take it and cherish it.

Secondly, I have a few things to say in my defence . . .

His clothes change so fast I can't keep up with what's what. So many times I've been sent upstairs to get 'a pair of leggings for him' and returned with what I consider to be a pair of leggings only to be informed that 'Oh no, Chris! Those are his smart/formal Sunday-morning social occasion leggings, I need his smart/CASUAL Tuesday-morning nursery leggings!' HOW THE FUCK WAS I MEANT TO KNOW THE DIFFERENCE?!

Also, literally the other day, I came downstairs with something I'd gotten out of his wardrobe and Rosie said, 'Oh, not them, I'm giving them to charity.' WHY WERE THEY IN THE WARDROBE THEN!?

Why does he have so many different bottles if he only likes drinking out of one? Get rid of the rest.

And I didn't mean I thought you liked it . . . I meant you like MOANING ABOUT IT!

Sadly I have to take the rest on the chin. It's too much. If it was up to me he'd have multiple sets of the EXACT same clothes . . . like Peter Griffin or Bart Simpson.

God, I hope I die first. Fingers crossed!

One thing I often think about is who will be left alive last and thus be the biggest pain in the arse to Robin and his family? (I always think about happy stuff.)

Know what I mean? I often think I'd rather die in an accident when I was really old than fade away into not knowing who people are and needing my arse wiped. Knowing that with every motion of scraping shit from my rotting old anus, Robin or his wife or husband are just thinking, 'Will you just hurry up and die so we can have your fucking house!' Is that too grim? It's just a thought I have sometimes. I wouldn't want to be a burden. Or if I was a burden, I would hope they were happy to shoulder that burden. Or . . .

I could go full *Saw* and I could set up some kind of Bond villain-esque scheme where the longer they keep me alive the more money they get from my estate. But it all goes into a secret offshore bank account that they can't access until I'm dead. A bit more goes in each month and then if they keep me alive past my pre-decided death age they get all the rest too. But shit, what if they get to a certain amount and they think, 'Fuck this, we've got enough money here, and his shits are getting claggier and more frequent – let's cash out!?!' Well, then I'll add in ANOTHER failsafe that if I don't get past a certain age, it ALL gets taken off them . . . I'll set this age at 90 and my previously mentioned death age for them to get it all will be set at 130. I'm sure people will be living longer by then.

Taking all of this into account, I think we can all agree it would be better for everyone if I die first . . . BUT I want to be buried with all of my money, and my surviving family members have to dig me up to get it. And when they open the coffin, it's empty and I suddenly emerge from behind a nearby tombstone and shout, 'SURPRISE, MOTHERFUCKERS! You were going to dig me up to get my money? Shame on you all! As a punishment I'm going for a shit and you're all coming to take turns wiping.'

You're playing too many computer games at the moment and it's showing, Chris.

Let's Talk about Shit

WARNING PAGE

WARNING! The following pages are not for the faint-hearted. If you are a regular listener to the podcast, you will know that we get sent so many horrifically graphic, disgusting faeces- and urine-based disaster stories that we had to give them their own section so as to contain them into a controlled portion of the podcast.

The moment we announced this book I was inundated with messages from people saying, 'There needs to be a specific section with the disgusting letters from the public', and I'm all about giving the people what they want.

Rosie is wholeheartedly against this idea and feels that as this is a book, it should be higher brow than the podcast . . . She thinks that the stories will be WORSE written down. And that's exactly why I'm insisting this section is included. It's got its own jingle, for fuck's sake! (A jingle that Rosie recorded herself, may I add!) You are now entering that section of the book.

It's what the people want! It's part of what we do. If this section wasn't here, it would be like when you go to see your favourite band and they just play a load of new studio tracks from their forthcoming album that no one has heard yet . . . and you stand there screaming, 'PLAY THE HITS, YOU BELL ENDS!'

However, if you are in the same boat as Rosie here, feel free to stop reading now. In fact, I've even gone one further and added a 'CUT HERE' line to all the pages in this section. You can snip them out and pretend this whole thing never happened . . . because toilet humour is clearly beneath you, YOUR MAJESTY!

I hope you've otherwise enjoyed yourself during this book. Farewell, all the best, nice chatting with you, have a lovely life.

Chris x

I'm serious, this is happening. Just go if it's not for you. It's going to be horrific.

Right . . . have they gone?

OK, good . . . let's do this!

I've kept everyone anonymous . . . Not all of them asked to be, because, well . . . as you'll see, some people are just disgusting and they don't even care. But I've spared them the humiliation of having their darkest secrets published openly, for all to read about.

I just want to clarify, I didn't want this section to be in the book. If you are at all upset, disgusted or offended, please blame Chris . . . Oh, and Penguin.

CUT HERE

Dear Chris and Rosie,

A few years ago, my wife and I had been travelling around New Zealand for a few weeks staying in motels and a couple of hostels. We had booked a few days in Fiji to give ourselves a nice little treat to end the holiday and I had booked us into a five-star hotel to really end it with a bang.

On one day, we went on a full-day boat trip to a deserted island to chill out on the beach, snorkel and drink the day away. When we got back to the mainland, we decided to go for dinner around the marina before heading back to the hotel for the night – which was about a 1.5-kilometre walk away.

Before we even left the restaurant, my stomach started making some strange gurgling noises, but I decided I'd rather get back to the room and have a shit in peace so we paid up and started the journey back.

Now the hotel and marina were part of a big complex including another ten or so hotels, a golf course and some shops, so the grounds were pretty big. To make it easy to get around everywhere, they had these things called Bula buses. These were essentially flatbed lorries with benches going along the length of them for people to sit down and face outwards on each side of the bus to take in the beautiful views.

There weren't any buses waiting to pick people up from the marina, and given how the gripes in my stomach were intensifying and the farts getting more and more pungent, I thought we had better walk back in the open air. About halfway through, the gripes intensified again and I had to start squeezing my bum cheeks together to avoiding shitting myself right there on the pavement. I couldn't even hold a conversation with my wife as all my effort was required to stop myself from farting and potentially evacuating my bowels before we got back to the room. I was dripping with sweat and having to breathe like a pregnant woman in labour with the effort.

As we rounded the last corner and the reception of our hotel came into view about 100 metres away, I began to feel some relief that the ordeal would soon be over. But I spoke too soon. The relief must have meant I momentarily relaxed my sphincter to let out a fart . . . but I felt myself begin to follow through. I immediately turned around and did the 'man quite clearly shitting himself' jog about 10 metres back to some bushes that separated the footpath from the road.

What added to the situation was that I was wearing boardies from the day on the boat, and in my frantic state, I was having issues untying the knot to pull them down. The shit was still streaming out of my clenched cheeks at this point but I tore the shorts down over my hips and squatted in the quiet, dark bushes and just let it go.

I shat for about one minute straight, quite loudly, but luckily no one was around and it was quite dark as it was night-time and there weren't really any streetlights to speak of.

After my wife's initial shock and concern – lasting no more than five seconds – she had begun to (figuratively) piss herself laughing at me. After she managed to catch her breath, I informed her that she'd need to go back to the hotel and get me a change of shorts.

She left to go and get me some shorts – still laughing – while I began to pick leaves off the bushes in an attempt to clean myself up. She says she ran back to the room but I think she took a leisurely walk instead.

After I had cleaned myself up as best I could, I kept squatting so I stayed within the cover of the thick bushes I was in.

At some point during this wait, I heard a vehicle coming up the road. I turned around and saw a Bula bus coming down the road to drop people off at our hotel. What I hadn't noticed before is that at night, the buses have floodlights pointing out the left and right side of the bus to light up the surrounding area. As the bus drove by, I was lit up like I was on stage at Wembley. It turns out the thick bush I thought I was hiding behind was a very thin layer of leaves that could easily be seen through when lit up with a floodlight. I turned my head away from the road because I couldn't bear to look the other tourists in the eye, but I heard some gasps as they drove by and clearly saw me.

I was about ready to die and just wanted my wife to get back with the change of clothes so I could go back to the room and empty the minibar to help me forget the evening.

It was here that it became evident that there had been some sort of traffic jam in the resort and the buses had backed up a bit. I turned around to see two more buses approaching, each full of tourists looking out at the lush green, floodlit landscape. Now our hotel was right at the tip of the peninsula and had a very narrow area to turn around, so only one bus could get to the entrance at a time and any others had to wait a short distance down the road. It turns out, the buses decided to wait right next to the bushes where I was waiting. As the first bus crawled up next to me, I was once again lit up and heard the tourists gasp in shock once again at seeing a feral man squatting over a big pile of shit without any shorts on. I couldn't avoid eye contact any longer so I slowly turned to see the people who were supposed to be looking out the other side of the bus had turned around and were also staring at me with open mouths. All I could do was mouth 'I'm so sorry' to them and look away again until they moved off. It felt like an eternity until the bus left but as soon as it did, the next one took its place in the 'waiting area' and I had to repeat the whole 'I'm sorry' thing again.

Eventually my wife returned with a beach
towel, a plastic bag and some new shorts –
her eyes were still streaming with tears as
she laughed at me. I wiped myself down with
the towel, put the new shorts on and loaded
up the plastic bag with a shitty beach towel
and my swimming shorts and began walking
the last 100 metres to the hotel.

To add insult to injury, because it was
dark, I hadn't noticed that shit had run
down my legs and left streaks from my arse
to my ankles which I hadn't managed to
ENTIRELY clean off. So I had to walk through
the lobby of this lovely five-star hotel
with legs covered in shit holding a plastic
bag of my shitty clothes. I didn't want to
draw any more unnecessary attention to
myself so I walked calmly and didn't run,
but I'm sure some of the people who were
just dropped off by the various Bula buses
noticed me and began making their way to the
front desk to complain that some guy was
just shitting in the bushes outside the
front of the hotel and was probably going to
do the same by the pool or something.

Needless to say, I got back to my room, had
a very, very long shower and drowned my
sorrows. I also had to avoid everyone else

during the last day in the hotel as I didn't
know who would recognize me from the night
before.

I haven't really told anyone about this so
I'd appreciate it if you could keep me
anonymous – aside from the twenty-five or so
people on the buses who saw me shit myself
too.

Cheers

I have to be honest here, I found this story AGES ago and realized it was just too long for the podcast, so the moment we got
signed up to do this book I dug it straight out of the email. What
a tragic tale.

Firstly, this story justifies my hatred of hostels. These people
literally had to book an actual hotel at the end of their string of
hostel stays so that the whole thing actually counted as a holiday. I love being right.

Now, I have a few things I'd like to pull out of this story. Firstly,
wonderfully written – you should look into maybe writing crime
thrillers or something. Secondly, the casual dropping in of 'man
quite clearly shitting himself jog' tells me that this isn't your first
rodeo, my friend. No, no, no . . . you've done this before. You're
a seasoned pro at shitting yourself.

As someone who (at the time of writing this) has never shat
myself in public . . . or in private since being a child, I don't think
I will ever understand the feeling of needing to run to a bloody
bush and go for it. It must genuinely be terrifying. But I bet it's

nowhere near as terrifying as seeing what is basically a floodlight-equipped tour bus coming at you as you nest in your shitty hedge with your dirty shorts round your ankles.

I wish they had had one of those tour guides with a microphone:

'The flora of Fiji comprises of hardwood trees, mangroves, bamboo and palms. If you look to your left you will see the tagimoucia, which is the national flower of Fiji, and if you look to your right you will see a defecating man who should have stayed in the shithole hostel down the road where he belongs.'

It's the wife laughing hysterically and taking ages to get him his clothes that I feel is the best thing in this whole story.

Also, imagine if you were just arriving on your honeymoon and there's a man outside shitting in the bush. Eeeeeh! Hilarious. Disgusting, yes, but very funny. This one isn't too bad, Chris. I don't mind this one. Hopefully they'll not get any worse than this.

Dear Chris and Rosie,

This story goes back to just over ten years ago. I was on my way to college and I'd slept in so I couldn't get my usual bus. Instead I had to get four buses (which weirdly took less time than just the one).

Anyway, the final leg of the journey, which should have been a quick five minutes, turned out to be THE longest and MOST disgusting five minutes of my life. I love toilet humour - but after this fiasco I could not eat for two days. I'm pretty sure I may have had nightmares.

While sitting diagonally behind a lady I noticed she was becoming very fidgety and a bit wriggly bummed down below. 'Odd,' I thought, 'but nowt as queer as folk.' Obviously I kept watching her because a) I'm a nosy fucker and b) I was concerned as to why she seemingly had ants in her pants. Was it the seats? Should I stand up? Were there bed bugs? Was I going to get an itchy bum? She finally settled at a funny angle and I went back to watching out the window.

The smell of shit then began to fill the bus. Now I'm not the brightest spark in the dictionary but I knew it was said lady. She had obviously positioned herself at an awkward angle to shit. While I was staring at her in horror, she then proceeded to put her hand down her trousers and produce said shit. I swear I saw some sweetcorn in there. And sat with it in her hand. She turned to see if anyone had noticed and made eye contact with me – who was sat in a state of utter shock. I looked at her, she looked at me, we looked at the shit and back to each other again. She then proceeded to put the shit BACK IN HER PANTS and just sat with her hand held up in front of her smeared with her stinky shite. It was at this point I began to cry. I disembarked the bus and ran into college to tell my friends about it while they were all tucking into their sausage sandwiches. As I said, I never ate for two days. And I think I may not eat again for another two days from revisiting this tale.

Lots of love,

Proudy xx

'Not the brightest spark in the dictionary' – classic.

This is horrific. Literally horrific. This is what I mean when I say on the podcast that WE are all the victims of these stories. This is not me here shovelling this into your face, dear reader, and laughing my head off at your reaction. I AM THE VICTIM TOO! I just had to read that as well.

Can I speak for everyone when I say 'WHY DIDN'T YOU STAY TO SEE WHAT HAPPENED?!' Where did she get off? Where did she go? Did she pop it in the bin? Did she wash her hands? (Of course she fucking didn't.) No wonder there has been a pandemic.

Why did she get it out of her pants? For the love of God, leave it there. Look, we all turn round and have a little look into the toilet after we've finished. Don't lie. You do. We all do. It's nice to see what you've made . . . see what all the fuss is about. But there is no way I would ever pick it up. Was she surprised?! Did she think, 'Oh, my purse is a bit warm – HOLD ON, THAT'S NOT MY PURSE!' People are disgusting. I bet she pressed the button to stop the bus with her dirty hand too.

This is why I don't like getting on public transport. This right here. I'd rather walk.

Hello,

Loving the podcast! I work in a supermarket and a co-worker told me this horrific poo story that I had to share. So one day she needed the toilet and decided to nip to the customer toilets instead of the staff toilets because it was quicker. She went into the stall and the entire thing was covered in poo. The walls were covered, there were poo footprints on the floor - not only that, but it was actually smudged in, as if someone had got their hands and rubbed it into the walls/toilet seat. She came out of the toilet and found the cleaner and all she said was, 'Oh yeah, they do that every week in the same stall.' They can't figure out who it is, but every single week someone comes in and smudges poo into the exact same stall.

That is all! Enjoy!

Rebecca x

Sorry, WHAT!?

Who does that?! Every week!? Tell me where this shop is and I'm coming to stake the place out and find this beast. Shocking behaviour. This has to be some kind of sexual thing. If they get there and their preferred stall is taken, do they wait?

God bless the public toilet cleaners of this world. Bless them! They deserve a lot more money than they get.

Do you know kids who wipe snot on walls and don't get told off by their parents? Well, this is what they become. The poor bloody cleaner! They need to put a camera up. I bet it's someone who works there performing a daily dirty protest!

Hi Rosie and Chris,

My dad owns a boat that you can sleep on and it's moored on a coast somewhere in Europe. (I know what you're thinking, bluddey posh people. Well, I promise you we're not posh and I'm sure after reading this you'll agree that boat or not, we're all just filthy animals.)

Anyway, this boat has two toilets on board. They cannot be flushed when the boat is docked in a marina or when we're anchored up near a beach as the contents would muddy the waters and create a smelly marina or even worse, infect the water where people are swimming. On top of this they bluddey reek, so I avoid using them whenever possible and prefer to use the marina toilet block, especially for shitting. It goes without saying, I just wee in the sea.

Now and then we take voyages up or down the coast and travel to different towns, sometimes anchoring up at sea overnight if the journey is long. In terms of toilets, this means that sometimes it can be one or two days at sea which for me, a nervous pooer at the best of times, is not ideal. I tend to hold them in until I'm back on dry land as the thought of doing a poo in the onboard toilets and just having it there looking at me until we can flush the toilets is just too awful.

One year we were halfway through a voyage when we decided to anchor up in a bay with beaches and cliffs that were only accessible from the sea – no roads to it – it was deserted and paradise. Me and my younger sister decided to swim up to the cliffs and do some exploring. We climbed the rocks, saw some great views and had an all-round fun afternoon.

We got hungry so started to swim the roughly 800-metre swim back to the boat for lunch. Unfortunately, spending a couple of hours on dry land seemed to trick my body into thinking we were in safe territory and close to a flushing toilet, and as I got back in the water I felt an unstoppable urge to poo. I tried to ignore it and keep swimming but each time I moved it just got stronger. I started to panic. We were already a fair distance from the beach (where there were no toilets anyway) and still quite a way from the boat. I started to slow down my swimming as each kick felt like it was pushing the poo further towards the exit. My little sister was ahead and looked back, confused, as I'm normally a fast swimmer. 'You OK?' she shouted.

'Yeah, just got a bit of cramp. I'm still coming, just slowly. See you back at the boat,' I replied.

Looking around to check if the coast was clear, I realized I was indeed alone. Would it be the worst thing in the world to pull down my bikini bottoms and poo? Fish poo in the sea all the time, I thought to myself. But how would I get the angle right and still stay afloat without drowning? These thoughts raced around my head for a few seconds before the desire to push got too strong. I pulled my bikini bottoms down to my knees and adopted a very deep squat, grasping my knees to try and stay balanced and afloat.

With one massive push my poo slipped out – the relief!! I swam ahead to my sister, not even checking to make sure it had disappeared. This was, definitely, a mistake . . .

I caught up to my sister and we chatted while swimming the last bit of the journey. I took a quick look back just to make sure

all was OK and made a horrendous
discovery . . .

Unfortunately I hadn't realized that we were
swimming down-current of the spot where I
had pooed. And my poo must have been a
floater. Floating not two feet behind my
sister's head was my massive turd. It must
have been so compact from being held in too
long as it hadn't disintegrated at all – it
was still fully intact, just bobbing along
behind us. In horror I panicked – what could
I do?!

In my flurry of thoughts I just screamed,
'Agghhhh, JELLYFISH!! Don't look back, just
swim away!!' Luckily my sister was so
terrified of them she believed me without a
backwards look and we both sped back to the
boat as fast as we could. Thankfully the
turd did not follow the same course as us
and we didn't have to watch it float by as
we were eating our lunch – my sister is none
the wiser and I still can't quite believe I
got away with it.

Now that I'm older I don't holiday with my
parents for such a long time so thankfully
I've never again had to go such a long time
without a flushing toilet.

Please for obvious reasons keep me
anonymous, although I'm sure if my sister
ever hears this it won't be too difficult
for her to join the dots . . .

Oh, how the other half live!

I've never read a story in my life that I can relate to less than this. It might as well have been written by an alien. I have no frames of reference for this other than 800 metres is a ridiculously long way to swim in the sea. Have you even seen the movie *Open Water*?

This was basically a posh remake of that scene in *Kevin & Perry Go Large* where Perry tries to fart in the sea. You should be arrested for international piracy and polluting the water. But mainly I'm just jealous of your boat . . . toilet issues aside.

What if it wasn't her poo, but another swimmer's which had caught up to them quicker than her own?

Also, I think I'd poo myself out of sheer excitement if my family owned a boat! Pure luxury! Forget about a caravan, Chris, what I really need is a boat!!

Chris and Rosie,

I've got four shit stories for you - you can
decide which, if any or even all you want to
broadcast. I'm a 52-year-old father of
four . . . these sadly are stories from
within the last ten to fifteen years. To

make matters worse, if they can be, my wife is utterly poo-phobic!!!!

Story 1

On a skiing holiday in the French Alps, a long enforced lunch due to 'white-out' was ended prematurely due to rumblings in my stomach. I mentioned to my wife that we ought to leave and walk back to the hotel as I needed the loo. Walking up the hill approximately 100 metres from the hotel, the pain intensified; I farted long and loudly and the floodgates opened. Uncontrollably. Shit flowed down the back of the only pair of jeans I had for the week. Standing still, pretending to check out the view, I took my hoodie off and wrapped it round my waist to conceal the expanding patch of liquid shit. My wife Nicola noticed the flow and offered me a 'fruit chew' to take my mind off the shit! This made me laugh out loud and another bowelful emptied into my pants. I shuffled up the hill, into the hotel reception, and with the look of a wild animal on my face looked for the lift to take me up to the room. As we exited the lift - rumblings; gas and shit flowed again . . . ! To my shock and relief there

was a toilet next to the lift. I managed to
shuffle in and pulled down my pants but as I
began to sit down it squirted out of me
again; over the cistern, wall and floor. My
pants were full; my trousers were full and
the room a stinking mess. I used my mobile
to call Nic and pleaded for more toilet roll
and a packet or two of wipes to try and
clean myself up.

I did manage to clean up the toilet –
just. I put my pants and jeans in a bag and
tied a knot - the smell was overpowering.
Problem was, I only had one pair of jeans
and a ski suit for the whole week. So I took
the bag down to the hotel reception and
asked them if they could launder my jeans.
The receptionist was just about to open the
bag to check on the dirty laundry when in a
panic I managed to stop her by telling her
not to as one of my children had had an
accident on my jeans . . . !

Story 2

I was waiting in a restaurant car park one
evening for my wife and children to turn up
for dinner. I'd had a bit of an upset stomach
that day and didn't feel too clean, so while
waiting in my car, I thought I'd drop my

pants and wipe my sore and slightly sticky arse. This I did but then (and I know it's wrong) I thought I'd wind the car window down and drop the wipes on the car park floor. As I did this I looked to the right and noticed a man in the car next to me . . . just shaking his head. He'd been watching me all the time.

Story 3

My 12-year-old daughter was in the kitchen sitting at the table watching TV. I needed a drink so walked into the kitchen - but then realized I probably need a poo. As I turned round to walk out and go to the loo, I farted. I was wearing shorts indoors - it was a warm day. Now I didn't shart . . . worse. A sticky, Malteser-shaped nugget rolled slowly down my right leg to the absolute horror of my daughter . . . my embarrassment was complete!

Story 4

During a particularly bad bout of upset stomach again, I'd retired to bed early - really quite tired. My wife came to bed a while after - I'm not sure when though as I was sound asleep.

At some point in the early hours I was awoken by a God-awful smell. I lifted the duvet to get out of bed and go to the loo as I'd obviously been farting but then realized I was sticky and covered in my own liquid shit from my knees up to my chest. I cried out loud to Nic: 'I've shat the bed!'

She very graciously helped me to the shower and changed the sheets.

Enjoy and laugh all you like.

Regards,

Matthew

My movie references are coming thick and fast here, but this is basically an email version of that scene in *The Goonies* where Chunk has been kidnapped and he just frantically tells the Fratellis every single bad thing he has ever done. We didn't need this outpouring (and by the sounds of it, neither did you) but thanks anyway!

Now I'm no health fanatic. I never preach about eating well and I can't remember the last time I had my five a day . . . or is it seven or eight now? Anyway, mate, you need to change your diet. To have four stories of shitting your pants to hand, ready to bash into an email to your favourite podcast, is not normal, mate. Eat some vegetables or something.

SH**GED. MARRIED. ANNOYED.

Jesus. I agree! I think he needs to go to the doctor's asap.

Imagine being single reading this? Single, lonely, looking for love and in fear of dying alone . . . then you see this guy is happily married to a long-suffering wife who by the sounds of things has to have wet wipes ON HAND for her constantly shitting man-toddler husband. What the hell must you think you are doing wrong? Using the toilet like a normal human?

WHO WIPES THEIR ARSE IN A CAR? Why would that enter your head?! And the poor bloke who saw the whole thing happen! What did he tell his family when he got home? You need house-training, man.

So this story blew my mind. I'm currently on a working holiday in Australia - lots of hostel life which I'm sure you're super jealous of.

Anyway . . . I'm currently living with a girl who told me this story:

She's from France and her friend in Lyon met a guy over Tinder or the French equivalent, went on a date, went back to his and really, really needed a shit.

So she went and then the flush was broken so she decided to just tell the guy, say sorry and ask him what she should do. He was really nice, told her not to worry and that

he would clean it; she insisted she would
but he refused to let her.

Five to ten minutes went by and he still
hadn't come back from the bathroom. She went
to find him and can you believe . . . she
found him EATING HER SHIT.

Apparently it's a fetish thing where he had
actually put laxatives in her meal on
purpose so that she could shit for him to
eat. Then after this she told other girls
she knew 'cause she was so freaked out, and
FIVE other girls she knew had experienced
something similar.

WHAT. THE. HELL.

Loads of love,

Sally

How many of you thought I'd put the same story in the book
twice? Tell the truth. I know how similar this is to the story in the
'Are We Vanilla?' section, and I've put it in here on purpose – to
show anyone who thinks these stories are made up that they
are in fact true. These two emails came in completely separately,
from different accounts and at different times of the year. Some
people are just the worst.

FIVE other girls. That's SEVEN if you add this writer and the
one from earlier on. I've said it before, and I will say it again,

many, many, MANY times before I leave this world . . . WHAT IS WRONG WITH PEOPLE!? Eating it?! NO! Why!?

I'm honestly in fear of breaking my exclamation mark key before this book is finished.

I knew this section was a mistake. People eating poo?! WHY?!?! We're never going to be a *Times* bestseller at this rate, Chris.

Hi Rosie and Chris,

Firstly I want to say I'm a police officer and I LOVE your podcast.

I probably have too many poo stories to mention . . . Dirty protests in cells where one guy was trying to write 'fuck the polis' on the cell walls but ran out of poo so only got to 'fuck the', for example.

But my favourite at the moment is AMAZING.

It didn't happen to me but a friend of mine . . . She's still horrified.

So my friend and her neighbour (in Scotland we call our partners in the police neighbours) jailed this girl who was absolutely steaming drunk and had been kicking off outside a club big time. She wouldn't take a telling and get up the road; she called my mate and her neighbour

everything - the usual charming insults
directed at cops.

They got her back to the police office and
before she was put in a cell she had to be
searched, including her handbag . . .
Standard practice . . .

On searching the handbag my pal pulls out a
huge wad of loo roll with something clearly
wrapped in it. By this time the girl who was
arrested was hysterically crying, all
upset . . .

So my pal unwraps the package . . . to
discover a giant poo.

She screams very unprofessionally and drops
the poo and it rolls down the cell
passageway.

A poor unsuspecting cop who's not involved
then walks through the door and stands in
it . . . Trailing poo all through the office.

It was chaos . . . Poo everywhere . . . The
office had to be closed for a deep clean and
all the prisoners had to be moved to another
office.

Turned out the girl who had been arrested
had been on a date at some lad's house

before she had gone into town and kicked off. She had gone to the bathroom and done a poo so big she couldn't flush it . . . Too embarrassed to tell the lad, she scooped it out and wrapped it up to dispose of later but FORGOT.

Please don't use my real name because I'll get into SOOOOO much bother . . . I'd like to be called Annabel . . . Dunno why.

Have a lovely week, you two x

Well, I'm not going to call you Annabel as it's just a bit creepy the way you said that . . .

Imagine walking down the corridor at work, almost at the end of your shift and standing in a random poo that had just rolled out of one of the rooms. I'd quit. There and then.

Can everyone stop shitting at strangers' houses, please? Can we just shit in our own homes or hotel rooms and be done with it? If you want to shit at my house, you better be staying over-night! Although to be fair, if you left immediately and took it with you I would actually be OK with it. Just let me open the door for you.

OH MY GOD, maybe she had a date in the past with the guy in the last story so she takes them all home now so no one eats them! Wow . . . this book has ruined me. As if that's where my brain went. I need a holiday.

I don't think I can read on if I'm honest. This is just awful.

If I HAD to comment on this I would just say, why didn't she get rid of the poo earlier? Flush it down the loo in the club? How do you forget you've got a shite in your handbag?!?! Bloody hell, man.

Hello Chris and Rosie,

I have a question: what lengths would you go to to help a family member out?

When my sister drinks alcohol she needs to have a poo. Doesn't matter where she is, as soon as alcohol touches her lips she feels the twinge coming on.

This particular night, she was in a night-club, the feeling to go was well and truly on the way as she rushed to the toilet to explode . . . Then her worst fears happened. No toilet roll. The quick thinker took her knickers off and began to wipe . . . This wasn't enough, she needed more, so she called my cousin from in the nightclub and asked her to take her knickers off. Sure enough, the kind family member did, she cleaned herself up then they went on their merry way and continued with their night.

Would you do the same??

Anon from Essex xx

Not a fucking chance. I wouldn't go out with her. Not unless I had evidence that she had evacuated her bowels before leaving the house. And no way are we eating while we're out. You can't enjoy your night properly if you're just waiting for the inevitable to happen.

'Shall we go to that lovely bar down on the river next?'

'Can't, mate, it's a ten-minute walk and the ticking shit time bomb over here might go off.'

Leave her at home.

Then again, I might have a solution ... You know how you can have pre-drinks in the house while you're getting ready? She should have hers sitting on the toilet. Music on, talking to you through the door or something, maybe even pull a little table up and a mirror so she can do her make-up while sitting there. Then once she's done, phone the taxi!

In her defence, I think she might have an allergy to alcohol? Maybe she should try a different drink? My friend Angela gets really poorly after drinking white wine. She doesn't shit herself while we're out, thank God! But she does get hay fever-like symptoms the next day, bless her.

Re the lending of knickers ... I'm not a hundred per cent I'd be up for that, but I'm always happy to help my fellow friends out. I did one time give a stranger my brand-new cardigan in a pub toilet once, as the zip on her dress popped open at the back and exposed her bare bum. I felt satisfied at my good deed at the time. Unfortunately it wasn't until I'd sobered up the next day that I was devastated as it really was a lovely cardigan. She never did try to get in touch with me to give it back either. Gutted, I was.

My fiancée is a huge fan of your podcast and I often listen along.

Hearing the 'let's talk about shit' segment has unearthed a memory which I had buried deep inside due to my trauma. I am now a pastor in a fairly large church so it really would be best to keep this anonymous.

A few years ago I had just started dating a girl when I made my first visit to her house. All was going well until I began to have severe stomach pain. Little did I know that this was to be the beginning of a very unpleasant IBS journey. Not knowing what to do, I asked my new girlfriend where the toilet was. She explained that I needed to go upstairs and that to get to the only toilet in the house you had to go through another room. After navigating my way through the house, I experienced what can only be described as a violent eruption from my rear end which continued for a good twenty minutes. Once the storm had passed, I realized that the ventilation in the bathroom was very limited. I desperately tried to find some sort of spray in the cupboards to reduce the potent smell I had produced, but with no luck. I decided the best course of action would be to leave the room with the door open, and hope that the smell would go unnoticed.

To my horror, when I opened the door I realized that in my rush to reach the toilet I hadn't noticed that the room I had gone through was in fact a bedroom, and the bedroom was now occupied. I stood in disbelief as I looked into the eyes of my girlfriend's parents, who I had not met before and only recognized from an earlier Facebook stalk. They were naked.

In a last bid to make a good impression, I introduced myself and said it was lovely to meet them as they cowered under the duvet trying to keep their dignity. I now realize it would perhaps have been best to leave as quickly as possible.

Knowing that diarrhoea never strikes just once, I sent a panicked text to my best mate, who called me and pretended he needed me for an emergency. I ran out of the house absolutely mortified.

I didn't ever tell my girlfriend this story. We only stayed together for a few months. But whenever I visited her house after that fateful day, I relieved myself in the garden like a dog.

Hope this finds you well.

I have to flag at this point that this email was titled 'PLEASE KEEP ME ANONYMOUS. I WORK IN A CHURCH' – genius.

I have to say it serves them right for only having an en suite. Either turn that bad lad into a toilet that is accessible from the rest of the house, or be prepared to have shitting strangers commuting through your room like it's King's Cross Station ... You probably didn't have to stop and introduce yourself, like.

'HI! So nice to meet you finally. I've heard so much about you, and I'm sure you could SMELL me from the fucking landing!'

This is similar to when people have toilets off kitchens at the rear of the house. It always makes for very uncomfortable pooing situations. I feel for him, I really do.

Hello Rosie and Chris,

I have a story for you both that I think you might enjoy!

I am a secondary school teacher. Once a week I have a Friday afternoon off in order to do my lesson planning.

However, one week, during this time, I was asked, very politely I must add, to cover a colleague's science lesson (despite this not being my area of expertise) because she had to leave unexpectedly during the day. I later found out that she had been suddenly struck down with diarrhoea and vomiting.

This had also been a common theme throughout the week amongst staff being ill in a similar way (I heavily suspect the home cooking that was brought into the staff room, naming no names, W E N D Y . . .).

Anyhow, I happily obliged as it was a class of well-behaved 11- to 12-year-olds, so easy enough, you would think.

How wrong I was . . .

Halfway through the lesson I felt the gurgle in my gut, and I knew I was in trouble. I could not leave the children alone in the lab during an experiment and anyway, the staff toilets were too far away in a different school block and building . . .

I spent the next fifteen/twenty minutes just whizzing around the science lab on the office chair from behind the desk, as I knew standing up would worsen the situation. Turns out I didn't need to stand up for that to happen . . .

I was clenching, I had sweat rolling down my face, and I was visibly shaking as I tried to hold back the inevitable rush of sewage. Children were asking me, 'Are you OK, Mr W?'

And I just half-smiled/half-grimaced it off with a nod until I could not stand it any longer . . .

I was in the middle of the classroom still on my wheelie
chair when the torrent was unleashed. The smell hit me instantly and I immediately threw up into one of the sinks, but no children spotted this! They did, however, take great notice of the smell, with cries of 'Oi! Who's shit themselves?!' and 'Have you blocked the toilets AGAIN, Johnny?' Poor Johnny.

I quickly blamed it on the gas from the experiment they were carrying out and wheeled myself back to the desk where I sat for ten minutes anxiously waiting for the bell to ring for the end of the school day so that I could assess the damage.

After those ten anxious minutes, the bell did indeed ring and the kids shot out the door nearly as fast as I had shat myself earlier. I stood up and, horrified, saw what

I had done. My filth had soaked through my pants and my trousers into the CREAM-COLOURED wheelie office chair, leaving the biggest yellow and brown stain . . .

I tied my coat around my waist to cover the shit-stained arse of my light grey trousers and tentatively wheeled the chair into the corridor. I ran next door and swapped the chair with that of a colleague who, to put it in mild terms, I absolutely hate. Am I a bad person?

I ran through school like a greyhound and was in my car before any kid could say, 'LOOK AT THAT IDIOT TEACHER!'

I quit my job that night.

Many shitty thanks,

Mr W

Right, this might explain why so many of my teachers' classrooms absolutely stunk when I was at school . . . do they all just shit themselves now and then? It would explain a lot.

Saying that, it's a bloody good job you quit that night. Imagine trying to get any respect at all from a classroom of kids when they all know full well that you shat yourself once and wheeled round the classroom like a stinky Roomba. Imagine being a student and hearing that one of your teachers did this, and they still worked there? It would be like Christmas Day! Imagine getting them for a lesson, how happy you would be telling everyone:

'What you got this afternoon?'

'Mate, we've got double maths with Wright the Shite!'

I fear he or she may have wanted to stay anonymous, Chris . . . ?

My art teacher used to smoke matches in his cupboard. I'm now wondering if he did it to disguise any bodily fluid odours? Guess we'll never know.

Hello Chris and Rosie,

I am a massive fan of the podcast and after months of consideration I decided it's time to let you in on my most embarrassing story.

A few years ago, I was in the most pain ever. I was at my friend's one evening and felt the most gruelling pain of my life. The pain could only be described as what I thought labour would feel like. It was too extreme for period pain. I knew I was putting the beef on around my tummy but surely I wasn't pregnant?! I ruled out being in labour only because I hadn't had a shag in over a year.

After the night of hell, I knew I had to go to hospital. As previously described, I hadn't had a shag in a while so got myself dressed up to go to hospital to pull a fit

doctor. My heart was racing when I saw the
Greek god of a doctor approaching my bed. It
was like I was in a Mills & Boon novel, I
honestly thought I was going to meet my
prince.

He asked the standard questions, THEN he asked
the question I hadn't even considered . . .
when was the last time I went to the toilet?
Not going to lie, I am absolutely not regular
at all. I suddenly realized that I had most
definitely missed my weekly poo schedule. I
had to break the news to him; he had a little
feel of my belly that he described as swollen,
hence why I had been piling on the weight.
Everything clicked into place and I was so
mortified when he turned me over and FINGERED
MY ARSEHOLE. Not going to lie, it was the most
action I'd had in over a year so I wasn't
really too mad. Four enemas and a ridiculous
amount of laxatives later, they sent me home
as I still hadn't pooed.

A few days later, I still hadn't had my poo
but was taking laxatives each day to shit it
out when the time was right for it to make
an appearance. Sunday dinner at me nanna's.
Enjoying a lovely meal cooked by my little
nanna and I needed a little pump. Just as
everyone started tucking in, I prepared

myself for a dainty little silent pump. It wasn't - it was pure shitty water flooding from my arse. There was no stopping this literal shitmix of enemas and laxatives that had been brewing for days. My jeans were soaked through, there was a puddle of shitty water pouring from the chair down on to the floor and I ruined Sunday dinner.

No one knew what to say or how to act other than my mam shouting at me to get in the shower and get changed into a clean towel. As I emerged from the bathroom, my mam was waiting to take me home in her car. The car was covered with towels and bin liners as well as the towel wrapped around my waist.

Although this story is long and traumatic, what I take from it is that the sexiest doctor in the North East fingered my arsehole, so every cloud, eh?

PS. Please keep me anonymous. I am a changed woman and I am still hunting for my future husband.

You need to be put in prison for attempting to knock a silent fart out just as everyone is sitting down for Sunday dinner, you fucking animal. Next time you should eat yours in the kitchen on the floor with the dog! Shocking behaviour, that.

Secondly, as a man who was once constipated for a week and a half, I feel your pain. This story is remarkably similar to when it happened to me (minus defecating all over my gran's dining room and having to be taken home in a car that looks like Dexter is about to chop someone up in it).

I had an enema and laxatives and they did nothing. I was told by a comedy promoter I was working with at the time that prune juice would help, so I drank a LITRE of the stuff, in one go. A LITRE. You know what happens when you drink a litre of prune juice? You shit a litre of prune juice! It somehow circumnavigates the blockage and comes out almost ready to go straight back into the bottle. Probably wouldn't affect the flavour, to be fair, as prune juice already tastes like it's been filtered through the bowels of a thousand dogs.

Chris, man!!

I went to a walk-in-centre as I was living in Manchester at the time and my GP was still in South Shields. I can't comment on the attractiveness of the doctor as he was a very old man and was just furious that he had to put his finger in my bum. Something which I do not like, at all, in any way, shape or form, so I was clenching. He kept shouting at me to relax, failing to spot the irony that screaming 'RELAX' while rolling his sleeves up further and applying more pressure to my terrified arse would get exactly the opposite effect. He just got madder and madder . . . I think it was because I nipped his finger.

In the end I had to go for a colonic. It was terrifying and magical at the same time. They fill you up with water from the arse until your stomach feels like it's going to explode then deflate you again and again like they are rinsing out a shit-filled waterbed. You get a weird buzz when they are done as all the toxins leave your body, and you feel like you might just be able to fly as you're about three stone lighter. It was cool, but I've never had once since, and that was ten years ago. It was the small talk that I had to make with the lady doing it that I found weird.

I found her on Google and she boasted that she had a 'private colonic irrigation clinic'. Word to the wise, 'private colonic irrigation clinic' can sometimes just mean 'house'. She was basically saying, 'Come to my house and let me put a tube up your arse in my spare bedroom while my family are all in the house.' No lie, I could hear her kids playing on the Xbox in the next room. I just drink a shitload of water these days and that seems to keep everything moving. There we go, we've all learnt something here!

HOW DID I NOT KNOW THAT IT WAS AT HER HOUSE?!? That brings a whole new level to the colonic story. I've always wanted to try one, to be honest, but I'm pretty regular as you know, Chris. And now all of you reading. Sorry about that.

Dear Rosie and Chris,

Obsessed with your podcast, actually count down to when the next one comes out! So good!

I'm also really pleased you started the poo segment. I have far too many stories of wetting and shitting myself, but I thought this was golden . . .

When I was 20 (I'm 24 now), I had quite the poo nightmare . . .

What you need to know is that I was wearing floaty shorts and very little underwear underneath . . . I bent over to get something out of the oven and went for the fart, or so I thought. Turns out I had rather a funny tummy and, without realizing, a poo the size of my fist was lying on the kitchen floor . . . with my sister and mum both in the room (and both somehow missed this situation). I decided to abandon my food, run to the loo, clean myself up and then blame it on the dogs when I got back.

As I went to leave the room I looked back to see if it was a mess I could blame on the dog only to see THE DOG WAS LICKING UP MY POO AND CLEANING EVERY OUNCE OF IT FOR ME.

She was a very loyal dog . . . no longer with us (whether my poo killed her I don't know), but I will always remember her as the poo licker and my saviour!

Please keep me anonymous, the family still
don't know about this one . . .

OH. MY. GOD.

Oh my Dog . . .

You just know later that night someone was sat watching TV letting that dog lick them all over the face. Shame on you! Shame on you for planning to let the dog take the blame in the first place, shame on you for letting the poor thing lick it all up and double shame on you for choosing to fart just as you were opening the oven! Firstly, it's disgusting, you're going to get poo particles on the food, and secondly, it's a fire hazard!

I'm more intrigued by the shorts situation. Just how floaty do your shorts need to be in order to let a poo fall out of your bottom and on to the floor? Very little underwear?! What does that mean? Crotchless knickers? Half a thong? Nothing at all?? I need details! I'm so confused by all of this!

Also, I'm sorry, Chris, but this right here is why we are never getting a dog.